Primary Mathematical Challenges

**PROBLEMS AND SOLUTIONS FROM
THE PRIMARY AND JUNIOR DIVISIONS
FOR THE YEARS 1995 TO 2001**

ISBN 0 9532786 3 8

The Scottish Mathematical Council

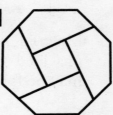

Contents

Copying of material from this book

Introduction

Mathematical Challenge, the problem-solving competition organised by the Scottish Mathematical Council, was introduced into Scottish secondary schools over 25 years ago. It has proved to be a very successful event and some of this success is due to the willingness of the organisers to allow the event to adapt to the needs of the users. One of these adaptations was to introduce, in the academic year 1995-1996, a primary strand. The purpose of this book is to make available the first six years of the questions and full solutions used with primary pupils and also questions used in the junior division. Many of the questions included appear in the books, *Mathematical Challenges III* and *Mathematical Challenges IV* published by the SMC. However, this book contains questions from the session 2000–2001 which have not appeared in the main series as yet.

In producing this book, the opportunity has been taken to make some minor corrections to the earlier published material and to try to offer solutions of a more accessible style. In many cases, alternative solutions are included where it is felt that they could perhaps enhance the mathematical knowledge of a reader.

As mentioned above, the event has evolved and continues to do so. Thus in this book, to give a more up-to-date picture of the event, the later years appear first and we work backwards to the session 1995-1996. The first section contains the 51 questions which have been made available to primary pupils, this is followed by the 39 questions which were set for the junior division but not used in primary schools. These are followed by the full solutions for all 90 questions. Those who are familiar with the competition will know that it is common for a question to be used for more than one group of pupils. This strategy is indicated by putting an asterisk after the number a questions to show that it was used by two groups of pupils, the lack of such a symbol indicates exclusive use of the question. So, for example, in 2000 – 2001, questions 1 and 2 were used only for primary pupils but question 3 was also used by pupils in the junior division,

Problem-solving can be a very satisfying activity but, as with many mathematical activities, the answer itself is by no means all that matters. The process of achieving the solution is at least as important as the answer itself. One aspect of mathematics which is often neglected is that of showing that, once an answer is arrived at, there are no more. In many cases, knowing why something is not an answer is extremely valuable. Finally, the solutions included are not necessarily the only valid ones so do not feel that others should be dismissed or valued less highly, just check them carefully.

Information about the SMC and its activities is available on the SMC website:
www.scot-maths.co.uk

March 2002

Section 1

Questions used in the Primary Division of Mathematical Challenges

2000 – 2001 Problems

1. There are three piles of £1 coins on a table. One has £11, another has £7 and the other has £6. The coins are to be moved so that each pile has £8.

   You can only add to a pile the same amount as it already contains and all the money you move must come from a single pile. For example, if a pile has £6 you may add £6 to it – no more, no less. How is this done?

   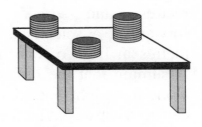

   Explain clearly how you arrived at your solution.

2. Find three 3-digit numbers that fulfil the following conditions:–
   - (i) all the digits from 1 to 9 must be used,
   - (ii) one of the numbers must be three times one of the other numbers,
   - (iii) the total of the three numbers must be 981.

   Explain clearly how you arrived at your solution.

3.* On a dark night, four travellers arrive at a difficult river crossing. The crossing is made over a rickety wooden bridge which only takes the weight of two people at a time. Each crossing must be accompanied by their only torch. Archie can cross in 3 minutes, Beth in 5 minutes, Carol in 9 minutes and David in 10 minutes. What is the shortest time in which all four can complete the crossing?

   Explain clearly how you arrived at your solution.

4. A new breed of rabbit has been discovered. Studying the rabbits, scientists discovered that they were only capable of jumping either 7 metres or 10 metres, and either backwards or forwards. A scientist places a carrot 8 metres in front of one of these rabbits. Assuming that the rabbit always moves along a straight line joining itself to the carrot, what would be the fewest number of jumps it would have to make in order to reach the carrot?

    Explain how you arrived at your answer.

5. Two boys, John and Mark, went for a walk and a picnic. On their way, they stopped at the village shop where John bought 3 big chocolate bars and Mark bought 4. On their walk, they met Liam who had no food with him. However, for their picnic they decided to share the chocolate bars equally among the three of them. When they returned, Liam found out at the village shop what the chocolate bars had cost. He said to the other two: 'Thank you for sharing the chocolate bars with me. I think that we should all pay equally for them.' He gave John and Mark a total of £3.50. How much did he give John and how much did he give Mark?

    Explain clearly how you arrived at your answer.

6. To cover a Christmas present (shown alongside) with sticky-backed paper, you will require six rectangular pieces. What are the dimensions of the smallest single rectangular piece of sticky backed paper from which you could cut out the six pieces with the minimum of wastage? **Explain your answer.**

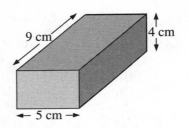

7. A positive whole number, greater than 1, is said to be a *polite number* if it can be expressed as the sum of consecutive whole numbers.

For example,   6 is polite because it is equal to 1 + 2 + 3;
                 10 is polite because 10 = 1 + 2 + 3 + 4;
                 7 is polite because 7 = 3 + 4.

Find all the polite numbers less than 21.
Find a pattern in the numbers that are **not** polite.
Explain why every odd number greater than 1 must be polite.

8.* A census-taker called at a house. He asked the woman living there the ages of her three children. The woman said 'The product of their ages is 72, and the sum of their ages is equal to the number on my front door which you can see.'

The census-taker replied, 'That is not enough information for me to calculate their ages.' What is the door number?
'Well my eldest child, in years, is presently learning to play chess' added the woman.
'Aha! Now I know their ages' said the census-taker, and left.
What were the children's ages?
Explain your reasoning.

9. (a) In the diagram alongside, the numbers 1, 2 and 3 have been filled in.
   Copy the diagram and put the numbers from 4 to 9 in the empty circles so that the numbers in the four circles on each side total 17.

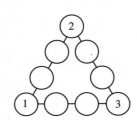

   (b) Draw a fresh diagram and arrange the numbers 1 to 9 in the circles so that each side totals 20. (This time, 1, 2 and 3 may not have to be at the vertices.)

1999 – 2000 Problems

1. Emma has only 10p, 20p and 50p coins in her purse. She has at least one 10p coin and at least three 20p coins. The total value of the coins is £5.60. What is the smallest possible number of coins she can have in her purse?
Explain fully how you arrived at your answer.

2. Yvonne has two brothers, Alan and Daryl. The product of the ages of all three children is 144. Alan is 11 years older than Daryl. How old is Yvonne?
Explain fully how you arrived at your answer.

3. A group of boys was picking apples. They each picked three apples. Then three other boys joined them. They wanted to share the picked apples equally among all the boys present but found that this was not possible. However, one of the boys picked one more apple. Now everyone could have exactly two apples. How many boys were there in the original group?

Explain fully how you arrived at your answer.

4. Find all the four digit numbers which (i) are divisible by 3, by 4 and by 5, and (ii) have 6 and 7 respectively for their first two digits, reading from the left.
Explain fully how you arrived at your answer.

5. In the number replacement puzzle below, each letter stands for a different digit.

$$\begin{array}{ccc} & A & B & C \\ - & & C & B \\ \hline & A & & C \end{array}$$

Can you find what digits A, B, C stand for?
Explain fully how you arrived at your answers.

6. Start with 1 2 3 4 5 6 7 8, insert plus signs to get $12 + 3 + 4 + 5 + 67 + 8$ and then work out the sum $12 + 3 + 4 + 5 + 67 + 8 = 99$. Find two other ways of obtaining the answer 99, again starting with 1 2 3 4 5 6 7 8 and inserting plus signs but no other symbols in each case. Can you obtain the answer if you start with 8 7 6 5 4 3 2 1 and insert only plus signs?

Explain fully how you arrived at your answer.

7. Eggs are placed in a 5 by 5 egg carton in such a way that there are at most 2 eggs in each row, at most 2 eggs in each column and at most 2 eggs in each of the two main diagonals (from the top left hand corner to the bottom right, and from the top right hand corner to the bottom left). What is the greatest number of eggs that can be placed in the carton?

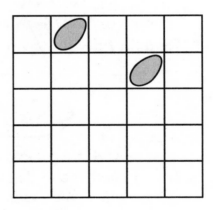

You should state the number and provide a diagram which clearly indicates the positions of the eggs.

(The diagram shows how two places might be occupied; do not assume that these places will be occupied in your diagram.)
Explain fully why there cannot be more eggs than the number shown in your diagram.

8.* The diagram shows a strange dartboard, in which the only scores available are 3, 6, 10 and 15. Suppose that you throw five darts, all of which land on the board and so each scores at least 3 points. Are the following total scores possible:

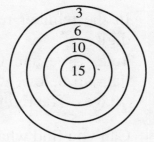

(i) 27,   (ii) 65,   (iii) 59?

In each case answer 'Yes' or 'No' and give your reasons.

9. You have six coins which all look exactly alike, but one of them is counterfeit. The genuine coins all weigh the same, but the counterfeit coin is lighter. You have a balance, so that you can compare the weights of the coins with one another, but you do not have weights. What is the smallest number of weighings which you will need to carry out in order to be sure of identifying the fake coin?

Explain fully the method you use.

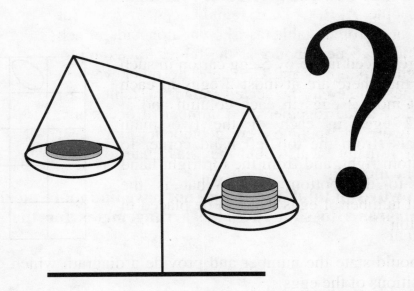

1998 – 1999 Problems

1. Aree, Bree and Cree are three villages near to each other, shown in the diagram below, where the straight lines represent the only roads joining the villages. The figures give the distances in kilometres between villages.

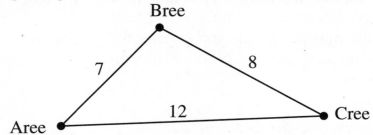

A new fire station is to be built to serve all three villages. It is to be on a roadside at such a position that the greatest distance that the fire-engine has to travel along the roads in an emergency at one of the villages is as small as it can be. Where should the fire station be positioned? You should show the position on a diagram, marking any distances clearly, and **explain why no other position is satisfactory.**

2.* Seven people, A, B, C, D, E, F and G can sit down for a meal at a round table as shown alongside. Each person has two neighbours at the table: for example, A's neighbours are B and G. There are other ways in which the people can be seated round the table. Last month they dined together on a number of occasions, and no two of the people were neighbours more than once. How many meals could they have had together during the month?

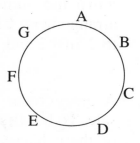

Explain why you think they could not have had more meals together and draw diagrams to show possible arrangements for the seating for all their meals.

3.* Emma and Harry have to dust all the ornaments (100 of them!) in their house every week. If Emma does it on her own it takes her 1 hour and 40 minutes. If Harry does it on his own it takes him 3 hours and 20 minutes. If they do it together how long will it take them? Give the length of time and **explain why they can complete the dusting in this time.**

4. There are 20 boys at a Halloween party and 9 of them are dressed as ghosts. Altogether 12 of the people at the party are dressed as ghosts and 5 people at the party are neither boys nor dressed as ghosts. Find out how many people there are at the party. Make sure that the number which you give is the only possible one, and **explain why you know this.**

5.* In the diagram, the number 5 is 'next to' 2, 3, 6 and 8, because the box occupied by 5 meets the boxes occupied by 2 (immediately above), by 3 (diagonally above and to the right), by 6 (immediately to the right) and by 8 (diagonally below and to the right). Similarly 4 is next to 1, 3, 6 and 7.

	1	
2	3	4
5	6	7
	8	

Draw a diagram in which the eight numbers in the boxes are rearranged, one in each box, so that no two consecutive numbers are next to each other. Write down the numbers next to 1, 2, 3, 4, 5, 6, 7 and 8 in turn in your new arrangement. Check carefully that 2 is not next to 1, that 1 and 3 are not next to 2, that 2 and 4 are not next to 3, and so on.

6.* A greengrocer had bags of apples for sale. To her first customer she sold half of these bags and half a bag. To her second customer she sold half of what was left and half a bag, and to her third customer she sold half of what was then left and half a bag. After this she had 3 bags left. Find out how many bags the greengrocer had at the beginning.

Check that your number is correct and that no other number is possible. Show your working.
[Please note: this problem can be solved without using algebra!]

7. Two calculations are 34 × 12 + 5 and 142 × 5 + 3. Both involve each of the digits 1, 2, 3, 4 and 5 once and only once, and each of the symbols × and + once and only once. Find the calculation of this kind which gives the biggest possible value, and **explain how you found it**.

The calculation must involve each of the digits 1, 2, 3, 4 and 5 once and only once, and each of the symbols × and + once and only once. No other symbols are to be used. The value of the calculation is the number obtained by carrying out the two operations: for example, the value of 34 × 12 + 5 = 413, because 34 × 12 = 408 and 408 + 5 = 413.

8.

A gardener has five days in which to plant out 200 flower beds. All the beds are the same shape and size. The gardener starts off slowly, but picks up speed. On each day after the first day, he planted twelve more flower beds than on the previous day, and he completed the task at the end of the fifth day. How many beds did he plant on the first day?
Explain your working.

9. The bus which I am about to catch is an 'exact-fare' bus, so that no change is given to passengers when they buy their tickets. I search the coins in my purse and find that I cannot make up the bus fare of £1 exactly. What is the largest sum of money I could have in my purse if I have no notes and no £2 coins?
Explain your working.

1997 – 1998 Problems

1.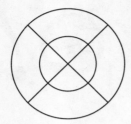

Figure 1

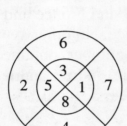

Figure 2

In figure 1, the two straight lines divide the inside of the larger circle into four parts. called *sectors*. Each sector has an *inner* part, which is inside the smaller circle, and an *outer* part, which is between the two circles.

In figure 2, the numbers 1 to 8 have been entered in the four sectors. Each sector contains two numbers, one in the inner part and one in the outer part: for example, the 'top' sector has 3 in the inner part and 6 in the outer part. The sums of the numbers in the four sectors are 3 + 6 = 9, 1 + 7 = 8, 8 + 4 = 12 and 5 + 2 = 7. The sum of the four numbers in the inner parts is 3 + 1 + 8 + 5 = 17 and the sum of the four numbers in the outer parts is 6 + 7 + 4 + 2 = 19. Find out whether the numbers 1 to 8 can be entered in figure 1 so that again there are two numbers in each sector, one in the inner part and one in the outer part, but now the sum of the two numbers in each sector is the same for all four sectors **and** the sum of the numbers in the four inner parts is the same as the sum of the numbers in the four outer parts.

Make sure that you show that you have checked your solution.

2.* In the sum shown, each digit 1, 2, 3, 4, 5, 6, 7, 8, 9 occurs just once.

$$
\begin{array}{r}
39 \\
45 \\
+\,78 \\
\hline
\text{Total} \quad 162 \\
\end{array}
$$

Is it possible to find similar sums, in which three 2-digit numbers are added together to give a 3-digit number and each digit 1, 2, 3, 4, 5, 6, 7, 8, 9 occurs just once,

     (i) when the total (the 3-digit number) is more than 200?

     (ii) when the total is more than 300?

In each case the answer should be 'Yes' or 'No'. If the answer is 'Yes', you should give an example of a sum satisfying the conditions. If the answer is 'No', you should explain why.

3.* A group of 20 scouts on holiday has hired 6 mountain bikes for 2 hours. Work out a scheme in which every scout rides on a bike for the same length of time, and all the bikes are ridden by the scouts continuously for the full two hour period.

Explain carefully how your scheme works.

(Please note: two or more scouts are not allowed to be on the same bike at the same time.)

4. The pages of a book are numbered consecutively: 1, 2, 3, 4 and so on. No pages are missing. If in the page numbers the digit 3 occurs exactly 99 times, what is the number of the last page?
Give reasons for your answer.

5.* I have a collection of Mathematical Challenge posters, all on A3 paper, so that they are rectangular in shape and have the same measurements. I have some drawing pins which I am going to use to pin the posters on my wall. Each poster must have a pin at each of its four corners, but adjacent posters can share a pin by allowing them to overlap slightly. I want to arrange them so that they cover a rectangular area of the wall, with their longer sides vertical.

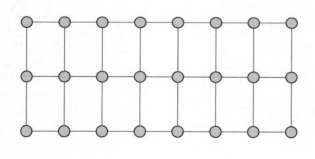
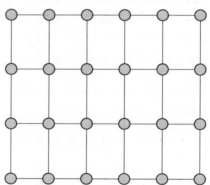

In the diagrams, 24 pins are used for 14 posters and 15 posters respectively. What is the greatest number of posters that I can pin up using 36 drawing pins?
Give reasons for your answer.

6. Today Jock and his son Wee Jock are both celebrating their birthdays. Jock is three times as old as Wee Jock. Some years from now, Jock will be twice as old as Wee Jock. How many times as old as he is now will Wee Jock be then?
Explain your answer.

7.* I start with the two whole numbers, 4 and 5, then add them to form a third:

$$4 + 5 = 9.$$

Now I multiply together all three numbers:

$$4 \times 5 \times 9 = 20 \times 9 = 180.$$

Now I add the three numbers together and multiply the result by 10:

$$4 + 5 + 9 = 18 \quad \text{and} \quad 18 \times 10 = 180,$$

so that the two answers are the same.

Find two other whole numbers which have the same property and **explain how you found them**. You must verify that when they are added together to give a third number, and all three numbers are then *multiplied* together, the answer is the same as the answer obtained by adding all three and then multiplying by 10.

8.* A large piece of cheese is shaped like a solid cylinder, as shown in diagram (i). A piece of wire is used to cut the cheese into smaller portions. First the cheese is placed with one of its circular ends on a board and then grooves are made with the wire across the other end. For example three grooves could be used, with positions as shown in diagram (ii).

(i)

The cuts are made using these grooves as guides; all the cuts are made straight down to the board. In the case illustrated, there will be 7 pieces of cheese after all the cuts have been completed.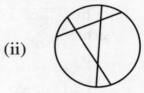

(ii)

Show by means of a diagram like (ii) how the cheese could be cut into 16 pieces using 5 grooves. The cuts must be completed from these grooves and no further grooves or cuts are to be used.

9.* In *Mathematical Challenge*, entrants are awarded a mark of 4 for a solution which is complete and correct, 3 for a good attempt which contains minor errors, 2 for a solution which contains more serious errors but is on the right lines, 1 for a solution showing a little progress or maybe an interesting idea, and 0 if there has been no worthwhile progress. (Occasionally a mark of 5 is awarded for an exceptionally good solution.)

For one of last year's questions, 100 entrants obtained a total of 289 marks for one of the problems. Nobody scored 5 and nobody scored 0, but 13 entrants were awarded 1 each and everyone else gained more than 1. Find (a) the *smallest* possible number of entrants who scored 4 marks, and (b) the *largest* possible number of entrants who scored 4 marks.

Explain your answers.

1996 – 1997 Problems

1. Colour the twelve small squares in the diagram, using three colours altogether, in such a way that

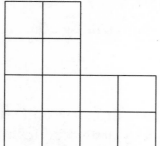

(a) no two squares which have an *edge* in common have the same colour

(b) each of the three colours is used in exactly four of the small squares,

(c) in any four small squares forming a square block as part of the diagram, all three colours are used.

(N. B. You must not mix the colours or use different colours in the same small square.)

2.* Anne, Boris, Coral and Damien are waiting to catch four different buses to go to their homes. 'Exact fare' is necessary on all the buses; the drivers take the money but do not give change. The four are horrified to discover that nobody has his or her exact fare. The coins they possess and the fares that they must pay are shown in the following table:

	20p	10p	5p	2p	1p	Fare required
Anne	0	0	2	2	0	13p
Boris	1	0	0	2	3	17p
Coral	1	0	1	0	1	22p
Damien	0	2	1	1	0	26p

Thus Anne has two 5p pieces and two 2p pieces. Can they exchange these coins amongst themselves in such a way that all can present their exact fares to their drivers? All the exchanges must be fair; nobody is allowed to gain any money, and so nobody can lose. As well as answering the question, **explain why you think that your answer is correct**.

3.* Jane and her dog Callum have a favourite walk in which they cover a total of 32 miles between them. On the outward journey, Callum runs four times as far as Jane walks, and on the return he covers twice the distance she does. Jane comes back by the same route as she followed on the outward journey. How far does she walk? **Explain why this is the distance Jane has covered.**

4.   In a magic triangle, the numbers 1, 2, 3, 4, 5, 6 are placed in the circles so that the sum of the numbers on each edge is the same. The triangle shown is magic because $1 + 6 + 2 = 9$, $1 + 5 + 3 = 9$ and $2 + 4 + 3 = 9$.

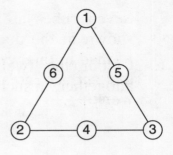

Find three other magic triangles, each with a different total, but still containing the numbers 1, 2, 3, 4, 5, 6. Say *why* they are magic triangles.

5.* You may already know the carol 'The twelve days of Christmas'. In case you don't, or have forgotten it, it starts like this:

'On the first day of Christmas, my true love sent to me: a *partridge* in a pear tree.

On the second day of Christmas, my true love sent to me: two *turtle doves* and a *partridge* in a pear tree.

On the third day of Christmas, my true love sent to me: three *French hens*, two *turtle doves* and a *partridge* in a pear tree.'

On the remaining days are added, day by day: 4 *colly birds*, 5 gold rings, 6 *geese* a-laying, 7 *swans* a-swimming, 8 maids a-milking, 9 ladies dancing, 10 lords a-leaping. 11 pipers playing, 12 drummers drumming. Thus on the fourth day the gifts are four *colly birds*, three *French hens*, two *turtle doves* and a *partridge* in a pear tree – and so it goes on.

How many *birds* did the true love send over the twelve days?
Show your working clearly.

6.* When Morag was one year old she was given a collection of gold coins. Her father said 'Did you know that

   when I divide the number of coins by 2 the remainder is 1.

   when I divide the number of coins by 3 the remainder is 2.

   when I divide the number of coins by 4 the remainder is 3.'

How many gold coins did Morag have when she was one year old? (Assume it is the smallest number of coins which satisfy all the conditions.)

Over the next few years, Morag was given more gold coins. When she was 12, her father noted that now he could still say all that he had said about the coins when Morag was one year old, but he could also say

   'When I divide the number of coins by 5 the remainder is 4.'

How many gold coins did Morag have then? (Again assume that it is the smallest number which satisfies all the conditions.)
Remember to explain your answers.

7. Seven cubes are glued together face to face as shown in the diagram. The volume of the solid formed in this way is 189 cubic centimetres. Find the surface area of the solid. **Explain your working.**

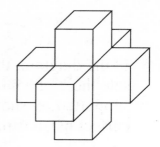

8.* Sarah and her young brother Stephen are earning pocket-money by mowing lawns for their neighbours. Sarah uses the lawn mower and hopes to make £5 an hour for herself. Stephen helps by taking away the cuttings and tidying up. They agree that he will receive 20% of the total payment made for doing the work.

It will take them four hours to mow the lawn in the garden of a large house nearby. How much will the owner pay if Sarah is to earn for herself exactly £5 an hour? **Explain your working.**

9.* In a game, you and a friend take turns to add on any number from 1 to 10, starting at 0. The winner is the first to say 100. For example, you start by adding 5 to 0 to get 5, then your friend adds 10 to 5 to get 15, then you add 1 to 15 to get 16, then your friend adds 4 to 16 to get 20, and so on.

Assuming that you start the game, but not necessarily as in the above example, how can you be sure to win? **Explain your system.**

1995 – 1996 Problems

1.* In the diagram, the top two sets of scales are in perfect balance. For the third set, the right hand side is heavier than the left hand side, and has to be supported as shown. What can be added to the left hand side to achieve a perfect balance in this case as well? **Explain your reasoning.**

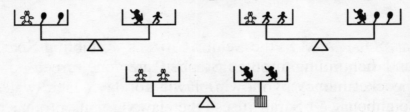

2.* Freddy the Fox, Gerry the Greyhound and Harry the Hare decided to have a race round a circular track. Terry the Tortoise was chosen to be referee and drew a white line across the track. From this they set off at 3.00p.m. Going at top speed, Freddy could complete a circuit of the track in 9 minutes, Gerry in 11 and Harry in 8. At 4.15p.m. Terry had had enough and decided that whoever crossed the white line next was the winner, no matter how many laps anyone had covered. Assuming that Freddy, Gerry and Harry all kept going at top speed for the whole of the period, determine who won the race. **Explain your answer.**

3.* Two planets Jo and Ko follow circular orbits round a star Agg as shown in the diagram. Each planet has constant speed, but their speeds are different; Jo takes 8 years to complete an orbit and Ko takes 24 years. At present, Agg, Jo and Ko are in a straight line. How many years will it be before they are next in a straight line? **Explain your reasoning.**

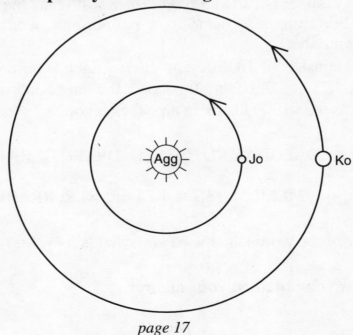

4.* The number 132 has three digits, no two of which are equal. It has the property of being equal to the sum of all the different 2-digit numbers made up from its three digits, viz.

$$132 = 13 + 12 + 21 + 23 + 31 + 32,$$

Find all other such 3-digit numbers and **explain how you found them.**

5.* Last year, S C R A M S, the Senior Citizens' Rambling Society, organised a short walking holiday in the Highlands. Everyone turned up on the first day, when the weather was hot. During the day, each walker covered the impressive distance of 18 miles. But this long walk produced sunburn and a crop of sprains and blisters, which led to an attendance of exactly 75% of the membership on the second day. On that day, those taking part covered 13 miles each, under cloudy skies and occasional downpours of sleety rain. The resulting shivers, coughs and sneezes led, on the third day, to a further reduction in numbers to exactly $\frac{2}{3}$ of the second day's total. This time the walk had to be abandoned when each participant had covered 9 miles, because the leader required treatment for a snake bite.

Fortunately everyone was well enough to attend the ceilidh on the evening of this third day, when the President proudly announced that despite the mishaps the total distance covered by members of the Society was between 1000 and 1100 miles. He had written down the exact figure on a piece of paper, but unfortunately he had lost this and in any case he wouldn't have been able to read it, because he had broken his glasses. What was the exact figure, and how many members did S C R A M S have last year? **Explain how you obtained your answer.**

6*. A word or a number is called a *palindrome* if it reads the same backwards as forwards. For example, 'radar' is a palindromic word and 1234321 is a palindromic number.

A codeword consists of 10 different letters. Each letter corresponds to one of the digits 0, 1, 2, ..., 9. Using this code, the ten palindromic perfect squares which are less than 100000 are, in alphabetical order

DAD, DAOAD, DEAED, DRMRD, LRARL,

MLMLM, MNM, REPER, RPR, RRLRR.

Which letter of the word is not used and what is its value?

Explain how you obtained your answer.

Section 2

Questions used in the
Junior Division of
Mathematical Challenges

2000 – 2001 Junior Problems

1. A non-stop train leaves London for Glasgow and travels at 80 miles per hour. At the same time, another non-stop train leaves Glasgow for London and travels at 60 miles per hour. How far apart are the trains a quarter of an hour before they pass one another?

2. The Annual General Meeting of the Price Fixing Club was about to begin when the Chairperson asked the Treasurer if every member present had paid his or her subscription. The Treasurer said 'Yes, but one member forgot all about the extra sum of £2.99 which we had requested from each member to enable us to buy a trophy. So the total sum that I collected was £399.00.' 'Very appropriate', said the Chairperson.
    Given that the club had fewer than 100 members, how many members were there?
    What was the annual subscription?

3.* Copy and complete the magic square alongside, where all rows, columns and diagonals add up to 111, in such a way that all the entries, apart from the given one, are prime numbers.

    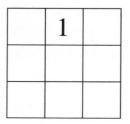

4.* What is the smallest integer greater than 1 which is a square, a cube and a fourth power?

5. You land on an alien planet and discover a mathematics school exercise book. The sums
    $$\underline{M} + \# + ✪ = ✪ + \# + ✪ + \# + ✪ = \# + \underline{M} + \# + \#$$
    have been marked as correct. From a picture, ||||| = $\underline{M}$, you deduce that $\underline{M} = 5$. Assuming that the + sign means the same on this planet as on Earth, and that they use the same numbers as we do but with different symbols, can you work out what digits ✪ and # stand for?

6. According to a book on astronomy for beginners, the Earth takes approximately 365·2564 days to complete one orbit round the sun. The planet Venus, which is closer to the sun, takes 224·643 days (Earth days!) to complete one orbit. Starting today, how long will it be before the Earth and Venus both complete whole numbers of orbits to within two days of one another?

7.* A chemist had 8 flasks capable of holding 12, 15, 27, 35, 37, 40, 53 and 69 fluid ounces respectively. He filled some with water and then filled all the rest **except one** with alcohol. He used exactly one and a half times as much alcohol as water.

   Which flask was left empty, which were filled with water and which with alcohol?

8.* We are given a collection of 2-digit prime numbers such that
   (i) the sum of the digits in each number is a 2-digit prime number,
   (ii) the sum of the original prime numbers is a prime number,
   (iii) the sum of the digits in the sum of the original prime numbers is a prime number. (The collection has at least two numbers in it.)

   Find two of the original prime numbers.

1999 – 2000 Junior Problems

1. In a recent election, 58335 votes were cast. The number of votes for the victorious candidate exceeded the numbers of votes for his three rivals by 569, 1772 and 2880 respectively. There were no spoilt voting papers. How many votes did each candidate receive?
    Explain your working.

2.* A pensioner lives next to a straight main road and he regularly walks to a newsagent's shop 2 km away along the road, to buy his morning paper. An express bus route uses the road, with a 30 minute service in both directions. It is a very reliable service; buses are never late and never early. They do not stop along this part of their route, but maintain a constant speed of 45 km per hour. Buses going in opposite directions pass one another at the shop. When the pensioner leaves home at 8 a.m., one of these buses passes him with both pensioner and bus going towards the shop; he is then half way between his home and the shop. He walks at a constant speed of 5 km per hour.

    One morning, the pensioner left home at 7.40 a.m. and walked to the shop at his usual speed. How many express buses passed him, going in the same direction as he was or in the opposite direction, between the time he left home and the time he arrived at the shop? For each of these buses, how far from his home was he when it passed him and in what direction was it travelling?
    Explain your working.

3.* A clock with a dial shows that the time is now 5 minutes to 2 o'clock.
    Calculate the angle between the hands of the clock.
    Assuming that the clock is going and is accurate, how many minutes will elapse before the angle between the hands next becomes 90 degrees?
    Explain your answers.
    (Solutions depending upon scale drawings are not acceptable.)

4. Eggs are placed in an 8 by 8 egg carton in such a way that there are at most 2 eggs in each row, at most 2 eggs in each column and at most 2 eggs in each of the two main diagonals (from the top left hand corner to the bottom right, and from the top right hand corner to the bottom left). What is the greatest number of eggs that can be placed in the carton?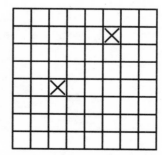

    You should state the number and provide a diagram which clearly indicates the positions of the eggs.

The diagram shows how two places might be occupied; do not assume that these places will be occupied in your diagram.
Explain fully why there cannot be more eggs than the number shown in your diagram.

5. The rector of a certain secondary school asked the head of the mathematics department how many good mathematical students there were in the school. On hearing the reply, he said 'You are much too demanding. I am sure that there are 50% more than that.' The teacher told her colleagues about the conversation. 'I think that the rector is wrong' said the youngest teacher. 'There are one third as many again as he said.' The oldest teacher disagreed. 'In my opinion, there are about one third of your figure', he said to the youngest teacher. 'So you and I differ by 12', he said to the head of department. What was the head of department's estimate?
Explain your solution in full.

6. A certain 7 digit number 1234***, where each * represents a missing digit, is a perfect square. Find its square root.
Explain your reasoning.

7.* You have twenty-five coins which all look exactly alike, but one of them is counterfeit. The genuine coins all weigh the same, but the counterfeit coin is lighter. You have a balance, so that you can compare the weights of the coins with one another, but you do not have weights. What is the smallest number of weighings which you will need to carry out in order to be sure of identifying the fake coin?
Explain fully the method you use.

1998 – 1999 Junior Problems

1.* How many 4-digit numbers are there using the digits 1, 3, 5, 7 once each? What is their sum?

How many 4-digit numbers can be made using these digits if any digit can be used more than once, and what is their sum?

Explain your answers.

2.* Catriona would like to become an Olympic sprinter. Her younger sister Morag would rather play football, but helps Catriona by racing against her. When they tried the 100 metre dash, Catriona crossed the winning line when Morag was still 20 metres short of it. Catriona wanted something more challenging, so it was agreed that she would start 20 metres behind the normal starting line. They both ran at exactly the same speeds as in the first race.

Where were Catriona and Morag when the winning line was crossed by whoever arrived at it first?

Explain your answer.

3.* Three soldiers have captured three opponents, and are taking them back to base. They must cross a wide river on the way, and this can only be done by using a small rowing boat, which can carry at most two people at a time. All three soldiers, but only one captive, can row. The soldiers decide that at no stage should there be more captives than soldiers at the same place, not even when getting in and out of the boat. Assuming that the captives cooperate with the soldiers, can all six people be transferred across the river? If your answer is 'Yes', you must explain how the process is carried out, giving full details. If your answer is 'No', you must explain why it is impossible for all six people to cross the river.

4.* John and I have house numbers which are both two-digit prime numbers and all four digits are different. If we add the house numbers together the resulting sum is made of two more different digits.

Curiously, the difference of our house numbers consists of two more different digits.

Stranger still, my sister's house number is also a two-digit prime number, which uses the remaining two digits. What is her house number?

Explain why you think that this number satisfies the conditions and why there is no other number which does this.

5.   A and B are whole numbers, both greater than 10. Their sum, A + B, is equal to 99. A is four times the sum of its own digits and B is seven times the sum of *its* own digits. Find A and B. **Explain your reasoning.**

6.* Here is a list of the squares of the whole numbers from 1 to 32 inclusive:

1	4	9	16	25	36	49	64
81	100	121	144	169	196	225	256
289	324	361	400	441	484	529	576
625	676	729	784	841	900	961	1024

Imagine the list being continued by adding 1089 ($= 33^2$), 1156 ($= 34^2$), 1225 ($= 35^2$) and so on. If you study the list, you will find that most of the numbers are mixtures of odd and even digits, but some have only even digits (for example 4, 64, 400, 484) and near the beginning of the list are the numbers 1 and 9, each consisting of just one odd digit. However, no other number amongst those shown consists entirely of odd digits.

Are there any squares of whole numbers, other than 1 and 9, which consist entirely of odd digits? Your answer should be either 'Yes' or 'No'. If your answer is 'Yes', you should give an example. If your answer is 'No', you should explain why there are no more squares consisting entirely of odd digits.

1997 – 1998 Junior Problems

1.

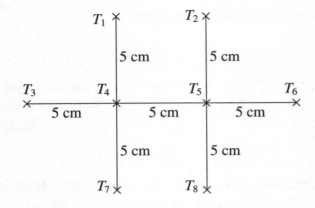

A wire grid is shown in the diagram on the left. Any point on a wire which is halfway between two other points on that wire has temperature halfway between the temperatures at these two points. The temperatures at the eight points indicated by × are denoted by T_1, T_2, T_3 and so on.

Each small section of the wire is 5 cm long.

Four of the temperatures are known: $T_3 = 2°$, $T_6 = 11°$ and $T_7 = T_8 = 0°$.
Find the unknown temperatures T_1, T_2, T_4 and T_5.
Give reasons for your answer.

2.*

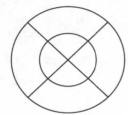

Figure 1

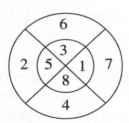

Figure 2

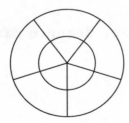

Figure 3

In figure 1, the two straight lines divide the inside of the larger circle into four parts, called *sectors*. Each sector has an *inner* part, which is inside the smaller circle, and an *outer* part, which is between the two circles.

In figure 2, the numbers 1 to 8 have been entered in the four sectors. Each sector contains two numbers, one in the inner part and one in the outer part; for example, the 'top' sector has 3 in the inner part and 6 in the outer part. The sums of the numbers in the four sectors are $3 + 6 = 9$, $1 + 7 = 8$, $8 + 4 = 12$ and $5 + 2 = 7$. The sum of the four numbers in the inner parts is $3 + 1 + 8 + 5 = 17$ and the sum of the four numbers in the outer parts is $6 + 7 + 4 + 2 = 19$. Find out whether the numbers 1 to 8 can be entered in figure 1 so that again there are two numbers in each sector, one in the inner part and one in the outer part, but now the sum of the two numbers in each sector is the same for all four sectors **and** the sum of the numbers in the four inner parts is the same as the sum of the numbers in the four outer parts. Make sure that you show that you have checked your solution.

Suppose that the inside of the larger circle is divided into five sectors, as in figure 3. Can you enter the numbers 1 to 10 in figure 3 so that there are two numbers in each sector, one in the inner part and one in the outer, the pairs in each sector adding up to the same number **and** the sum of the numbers in the five inner parts the same as the sum of the numbers in the five outer parts?
Give reasons for your answer.

3. When it is $\frac{1}{5}$ full of water, by weight, a jug weighs 560 grams. When it is $\frac{4}{5}$ full, the jug weighs 740 grams. What does the jug weigh when it is empty? **Give reasons for your answer.**

4. Great-Aunt Meg will soon be 90 years old. A family party is planned, and all her 259 descendants are still alive and hope to be there. You may not believe it, but only girls were born into the family! All Meg's daughters gave birth to the same number of children of their own, but this number was one less than the number of Meg's children. Then her grandchildren each gave birth to two less than the number of Meg's children. But so far her great-grandchildren are childless. How many children did Great-Aunt Meg have? **Explain your answer.**

5. The number 64152 is equal to the product $8 \times 9 \times 1 \times 891$. By considering the factors of 64152, find another way of expressing 64152 as the product of three 1-digit numbers and a 3-digit number formed from these digits. **Explain how you found your answer.**

6.* An astronaut is exploring the moon's surface with a moon buggy and two full 500 litre containers of fuel. The buggy's fuel tank has a capacity of 100 litres, but is currently empty. One litre of fuel is needed for every mile driven, whatever the circumstances. In addition, the buggy can carry at most one full fuel container. The astronaut must drive the buggy through all stages of the journey and at the end must be back at the starting point. In calculating the total distance that has been explored, any section of the journey covered more than once is counted only once.

What is the greatest distance that the astronaut can explore? **Explain how the route is followed and why no greater distance can be explored.**

1996 – 1997 Junior Problems

1.* One jug holds exactly 700ml of water when it is full, and another holds exactly 550 ml of water when it is full. A plentiful supply of water is available and both jugs can be filled as often as required. However, no other utensils are available. Explain how you would measure exactly 650 ml of water and say how you know that you could obtain this amount.

(Because of the shapes of the jugs, you cannot tell how much water either of them contains unless it is full.)

2.* A hiker dreamt that he was lost on a desolate moor and came upon a mysterious 'signpost'. What he read there seemed to him to be impossible, but happily for him his alarm clock went off and he awoke instantly. With the scene fresh in his mind (or so he thought) he wrote down what he remembered of the places and the numbers on the signpost:

AVOCH 44 BRACO 34 CARRICK 56 DALKEITH 70 EDZELL 58

Later he showed this to a friend and asked him if he could make sense of the numbers. The friend thought for a while and then said "You'd better go back to sleep and dream it again; one of the numbers is wrong." Explain how you think the numbers might be related to the names, and why the friend thought that one of them was wrong.

3.* The Town Hall clock was faulty. At twenty past three on Thursday afternoon, it showed 11.25. The faulty clock was in fact going backwards, covering 55 minutes in every hour as it did so. What time did it show at twenty past eight the following Saturday morning?

Give reasons for your answer. (Assume that the clock had a normal 12-hour dial.)

4. In a keenly fought by-election there were three serious candidates : Cathy Chatters, Bertie Braggs and Sally Smirks. All the other candidates expected, and received, only small numbers of votes.

On polling day the sun shone brightly and 75% of the electorate voted. Sally was the clear winner, because 60% of those voting supported her. Poor Bertie was supported by only 18% of the electorate, but did he fare better or worse than Cathy? Explain your answer.

5.* Radio Pop held a competition. Listeners were asked to place the following four groups in order of preference:

        Blare, The Howling Gaels, The Sleekit Beasties and Waterhole.

The organisers made their own choice; to win a place it was necessary to put the names in the order they had chosen. Jack suggested:

        The Howling Gaels, Blare, Waterhole, The Sleekit Beasties.

Only one of these was in the right place. Jill did better by choosing the order to be:

        Blare, Waterhole, The Sleekit Beasties and The Howling Gaels.

This gave exactly two groups in their correct places. In my entry, I put Waterhole and The Howling Gaels next to one another, but, in the organiser's choice, Waterhole and The Howling Gaels were not next to each other. What were the winning positions? Explain your reasoning.

6.* A railway company in Dragonia had to lay 350 metres of track. Sections of lengths 20 metres and 15 metres were available. For the 20 metre lengths, there was a fixed price of $500 each ($ stands for Dragonian dollars). However, for the 15 metre lengths, special rates were in force. Up to 3 cost $450 each, from 4 to 6 inclusive cost $425 each, from 7 to 9 inclusive cost $410 each, from 10 to 12 inclusive cost $390 each and 13 or more cost $380 each. Find the numbers of sections of the two kinds which should have been purchased by the company so that it bought exactly 350 metres of track at the least possible price. Explain your working.

1995 – 1996 Junior Problems

1.* My bank card has a four digit number code that I need to punch in when I get money out of the autoteller. To help me remember it I noted the following facts

    (a) No two digits are the same.

    (b) The fourth digit is the sum of the other three.

    (c) The first digit is the sum of the middle two digits.

    (d) If I reverse the number, the result is an exact multiple of 7.

What is the number of my bank card? Explain how you know what it is.

2.*

SUN	MON	TUES	WED	THURS	FRI	SAT
		1	2	3	4	5
6	7	8	9	10	11	12
13	14	15	16	17	18	19
20	21	22	23	24	25	26
27	28	29	30	31		

Show that the numbers in the 3×3 block displayed above can be rearranged to form a magic square. Can the numbers in any 3×3 block taken from one month in a calendar in this way be rearranged to form a magic square? Give your reasoning.

3.* Fred, Jane, Susan and Tom are manager, coach, captain and goalkeeper for a football team, not necessarily in that order.

    (a) Fred is the brother of the manager.

    (b) The coach and the manager are not related.

    (c) Susan is an only child.

    (d) The captain is older than Jane, but is in the same class.

    (e) Tom is in the same class as Susan.

    (f) The goalkeeper is not in the same class as Tom or Jane.

    (g) Jane is Susan's cousin.

    (h) Tom was disappointed not to be appointed coach.

Determine which person has which job, giving your reasons.

4. One year, less than 195 years ago, Christmas Day was on a Wednesday. How many Saturdays were there in December one hundred and five years later? Explain your answer.

5.*

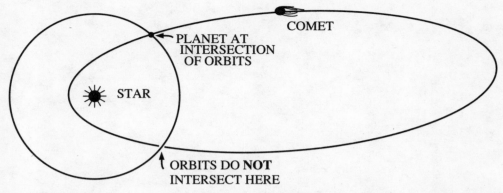

A planet takes 8 years to complete its orbit round a star. Concern is expressed because a comet, which takes 62 years to complete its orbit, is found to be following a path which intersects the path of the planet, as shown in the diagram. Calculation shows that the planet will next reach the place where the orbits meet three years before the comet is due to be there. When the comet reaches the intersection, the planet will of course have moved on in its orbit. Assuming that the planet and the comet continue to follow the same orbits, with no changes in the time taken, will they ever in the future reach the intersection of the orbits simultaneously, so that a collision will occur? Explain your reasoning.

6.* In our street, the houses are numbered consecutively from 1 upwards and my house is the one with the highest number. The square of my house number can be expressed as

    (i)   the sum of the squares of two of the house numbers,

    (ii) the sum of the squares of three of the house numbers,

    (iii) the sum of the squares of four of the house numbers,

    (iv) the sum of the squares of five of the house numbers,

    (v) the sum of the squares of six of the house numbers.

In these sums every house number except mine and Mr Brown's occurs at least once, eight house numbers occur at least twice, and no house number occurs more than once in any one sum. Find the number of Mr Brown's house, and explain how you found it.

Section 3

Solutions

2000 – 2001 Solutions

1. There are many possibilities. It is easier to follow the steps if the piles are labelled.

	Pile A	Pile B	Pile C
Initially	11 coins	7 coins	6 coins
Move 7 from A to B	4	14	6
Move 4 from C to A	8	14	2
Move 2 from B to C	8	12	4
Move 4 from B to C	8	8	8

2. Since the three numbers contain exactly nine digits, it follows that none of the digits can be repeated and the digit 0 cannot be involved. Any process to sort out this problem involves a lot of listing but, by taking note of the previous sentence, this can be managed more effectively. Below there is a list of all the valid 3-digit numbers and the result of multiplying each by 3. If this product is valid, they are added and their sum taken from 981.

123	369		145	435		167	501		189	567	225
124	372		146	438		168	504		192	576	213
125	375		147	441		169	507		193	579	
126	378	477	148	444		172	516		194	582	205
127	381		149	447		173	519		195	585	
128	384		152	456		174	522		196	588	
129	**387**	**465**	153	459		175	525		197	591	
132	396		154	462		176	528	277	198	594	
134	402		156	468		**178**	**534**	**269**	213	639	
135	405		157	471		179	537		214	642	
136	408	437	158	474		182	546	253	215	645	
137	411		159	477		183	549	249	216	648	
138	414		162	486		184	552		217	651	
139	417		163	489	329	185	555		218	654	109
142	426		164	492		186	558		219	657	105
143	429		165	495		187	561		231	693	

The rows highlighted are the ones in which the three numbers contain all 9 digits and satisfy all the conditions. So there are actually **two** valid solutions (although only one of them was needed to answer the question).

$$129 + 387 = 465 \quad \text{or} \quad 178 + 534 = 269.$$

[It may seem surprising that there are no more numbers in the list as it is given but remember that none of the numbers in the first column contain 0 nor does the same digit appear twice. The list can stop where it does because 231 + 693 = 924 which leaves a 2-digit answer when subtracted from 981.]

3. There must be at least five crossings.

    If Carol and David cross separately, their combined journeys take 19 minutes. There must be three other journeys and not all of them can be 3 minutes as any 3-minute journey is by Archie alone. So, if Carol and David cross separately, any complete crossing takes at least 30 minutes.

    If Carol and David do cross together, it cannot be the first crossing or the last crossing as, in these cases, Carol or David would have to cross three times making a total of 28 minutes for these three journeys alone. Thus Archie and Beth make the first crossing and there remain two possibilities with either Archie or Beth returning on the next crossing. Either possibilty takes 28 minutes which can be achieved as follows:

Crossing	Direction of travel		
1	→→→→→→→	Archie and Beth	5 minutes
2	←←←←←←←	Archie	3 minutes
3	→→→→→→→	Carol and David	10 minutes
4	←←←←←←←	Beth	5 minutes
5	→→→→→→→	Archie and Beth	5 minutes
		Total time	**28 minutes**

    The shortest time is 28 minutes.

4. To avoid wasting jumps, all the 7-metre jumps should be in one direction and all the 10-metre jumps must be in the other direction.

    First consider the 10-metre jumps to be forward. We need to find a number in the 10 times table which is 8 more than a number in the 7 times table. The multiples of 10 are 10, 20, 30, 40, 50 and $50 = 6 \times 7 + 8$ so the 8 metres can be reached with five forward jumps of 10 metres and six backward jumps of 7 metres. A total of eleven jumps.

    Now consider the 7-metre jumps to be forward. We need a number in the 7 times table which is 8 more than a number in the 10 times table. The multiples of 7 are 7, 14, 21, 28 and $28 = 2 \times 10 + 8$ so the 8 metres can be reached with four forward jumps of 7 metres and two backward jumps of 10 metres. A total of six jumps.

    As there are no other possibilities we can be sure that:

    The smallest number of jumps required is six.

5.   The three boys ate seven chocolate bars. Since Liam paid £3.50 for his share, the total cost was $3 \times £3.50 = £10.50$.   The cost of each bar was £10.50 ÷ 7 = £1.50. So, in the shop, John paid £4.50 and Mark £6 for their chocolate i.e.

   Liam gives John £1 and Mark £2.50 and so each pays £3.50.

6.   Because the covering is sticky-backed paper, there is no need to worry about the edges joining. We require two 9×5 pieces, two 9×4 pieces and two 5×4 pieces. The total area is therefore 202 cm^2.

   A rectangle measuring 9×23 i.e. 207 cm^2 gives one possible rectangular piece of paper with wastage 5 cm^2.

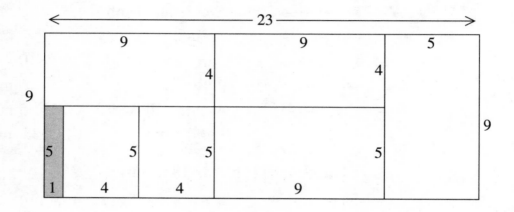

   Another arrangement using the same size of paper is

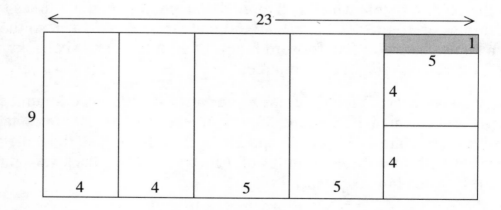

7.

$2 = 1 + 1$	not polite	$12 = 3 + 4 + 5$	polite
$3 = 2 + 1$	polite	$13 = 7 + 6$	polite
$4 = 3 + 1 = 2 + 2$	not polite	$14 = 2 + 3 + 4 + 5$	polite
$5 = 3 + 2$	polite	$15 = 8 + 7$	polite
$6 = 1 + 2 + 3$	polite	$16 = \ldots$	not polite
$7 = 4 + 3$	polite	$17 = 9 + 8$	polite
$8 = \ldots$	not polite	$18 = 5 + 6 + 7$	polite
$9 = 5 + 4$	polite	$19 = 10 + 9$	polite
$10 = 1 + 2 + 3 + 4$	polite	$20 = 6 + 5 + 4 + 3 + 2$	polite
$11 = 6 + 5$	polite		

The polite numbers less than 21 are

3, 5, 6, 7, 9, 10, 11, 12, 13, 14, 15, 17, 18, 19, 20.

The numbers which are not polite are 2, 4, 8, 16, ...
They double up each time.

An odd number is always polite. It can be written as two consecutive numbers added together. To get two such numbers, take 1 from the odd number then halve that number and add 1 back to one of the halves.

8. Since the question states that the product of the ages is 72, a good plan is to start by listing possible factors of 72. These are listed below with factors is ascending order and the sum of the factors in brackets.

$1 \times 1 \times 72$ [74] $1 \times 4 \times 18$ [23] $2 \times 2 \times 18$ [22] $2 \times 6 \times 6$ [14]
$1 \times 2 \times 36$ [39] $1 \times 6 \times 12$ [19] $2 \times 3 \times 12$ [17] $3 \times 3 \times 8$ [14]
$1 \times 3 \times 24$ [28] $1 \times 8 \times 9$ [18] $2 \times 4 \times 9$ [15] $3 \times 4 \times 6$ [13]

Since the census-taker cannot deduce the ages from the number of the house, **the house number must be the ambiguous case i.e. 14.**
The woman settles the matter by referring to her *eldest* child which eliminates the 2, 6, 6. **So the ages are 3, 3 and 8.**

9. (a) There is space for 9 numbers. The six which have not been used are 4, 5, 6, 7, 8, 9.
We need two numbers to go between the 1 and the 2 and add to give 14 so they will be either 6 and 8 or 5 and 9.
We need two numbers to go between the 1 and the 3 and add to give 13 so they will be 5 and 8 or 4 and 9 or 6 and 7.
We need two numbers to go between the 2 and the 3 and add to give 12 so they will be 4 and 8 or 5 and 7.

Putting 6 and 8 between the 1 and the 2 forces the 9 (and the 4) between the 1 and the 3 leaving the 5 and the 7 which works.

On the other hand, putting 5 and 9 between the 1 and the 2 forces the 6 (and the 7) between the 1 and the 3 leaving the 4 and the 8 which also works.

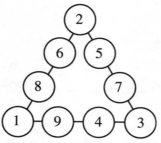
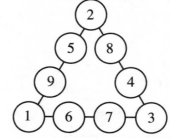

(b) In this case, the total of the three sides is 60. But the total of the numbers from 1 to 9 is only 45. The extra 15 must come from the corner numbers which are counted twice. So for the corners, we need three numbers which total 15. Possibilities are 2, 6, 7; 2, 5, 8; 2, 4, 9; 3, 4, 8; 3, 5, 7; 4, 5, 6; 1, 5, 9.

(i)   2, 6, 7 does not work because we have to have $6 + 3 + 4 + 7$ on one edge and that means that nothing will work between the 2 and the 7.

(ii) 2, 5, 8 does work $2 + 6 + 7 + 5$; $5 + 3 + 4 + 8$; $2 + 1 + 9 + 8$. (See A.) Also $2 + 4 + 9 + 5$; $2 + 3 + 7 + 8$; $5 + 1 + 6 + 8$.

(iii) 2, 4, 9 does not work because we have to have $2 + 6 + 8 + 4$ on one edge but $2 + \_ + \_ + 9$ fails as it needs 6 and 3 or 4 and 5.

(iv) 3, 4, 8 does not work because we have to have $3 + 6 + 7 + 4$; $3 + 2 + 9 + 8$ (or 8, 3 or 6, 5 – not available) $4 + \_ + \_ + 8$ needs 1, 7 or 2, 6 or 3, 5 which are not available.

(v)   3, 5, 7:– $3 + 4 + 8 + 5$; $3 + 1 + 9 + 7$ leaving $5 + 2 + 6 + 7$ so it works. (See B.)

(vi) 4, 5, 6:– $4 + 2 + 9 + 5$; $4 + 3 + 7 + 6$ and $5 + 1 + 8 + 6$ which works. (See C.)

:– or $4 + 3 + 8 + 5$; $4 + 1 + 9 + 6$ and $5 + 2 + 7 + 6$ which also works. (See D.)

(vii) 1, 5, 9:– $1 + 6 + 8 + 5$; $1 + 3 + 7 + 9$ which leaves $5 + 2 + 4 + 9$!

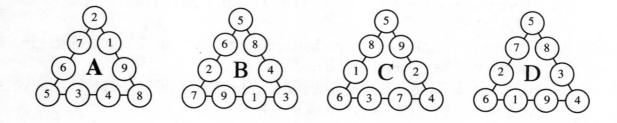

1999 – 2000 Solutions

1. Emma has to have the largest possible number of 50p coins.

   She cannot have ten 50p coins as that would make £5 and she has at least 70p in other coins.

   If she has nine 50p coins, she needs a further £1.10 which can be made up of five 20p pieces and one 10p. This gives a total of 15 coins.

   If she has less than nine 50p coins then the number of 20p and 10p coins will increase.

   Hence

   15 coins is the smallest.

2. The three ages have to multiply together to give 144. The factors of 144, in ascending order, are 1, 2, 3, 4, 6, 8, 9, 12, 16, 18, 24, 36, 48, 72, 144. It isn't difficult to see that the only factors in this list which differ by 11 are 1 and 12. So Daryl is 1 year old and Alan is 12 years old. To make the product of all three ages be 144,

   Yvonne is 12 years old.

   [A alternative is to write out a complete list of all the possible ages (some unrealistic)

$1 \times 1 \times 144$	$2 \times 2 \times 36$	$3 \times 3 \times 16$	$4 \times 4 \times 9$
$1 \times 2 \times 72$	$2 \times 3 \times 24$	$3 \times 4 \times 12$	$4 \times 6 \times 6$
$1 \times 3 \times 48$	$2 \times 4 \times 18$	$3 \times 6 \times 8$	
$1 \times 4 \times 36$	$2 \times 6 \times 12$		
$1 \times 6 \times 24$	$2 \times 8 \times 9$		
$1 \times 8 \times 18$			
$1 \times 9 \times 16$			
$1 \times 12 \times 12$			

   Now look for any in which two of the ages differ by 11. The only one is $1 \times 12 \times 12$. So Alan is 12, Daryl is 1 and Yvonne is 12.]

3. Between them, the extra three boys had six apples at the end. So five apples must have come from the original group (and one from the additional apple picked). Each boy in the original group must have given one apple to the extra boys. Since five apples were given, there must have been five boys who gave one apple each.

   So the original group contained five boys.

   Check: Five boys each with 3 apples gives 15 apples and one extra apple makes 16 apples. So when three boys join, there are eight boys and each will have 2 apples.

4. A number which can be divided exactly by 3 and by 4 can be divided exactly by $3 \times 4 = 12$. So, a number which can be divided exactly by 3 and by 4 and by 5 can be divided exactly by $3 \times 4 \times 5 = 60$. So we need to find multiples of 60 which are between 6700 and 6800. Since $6700 \div 60 = 111$ remainder 40, one possible number is $112 \times 60 = 6720$ and adding 60 to this gives a second value, 6780.

The only two possible numbers are 6720 and 6780.

5. Since there is no hundreds digit in the answer, $A = 1$.
In the units column, $C - B = C$ so $B = 0$. Which gives

$$\begin{array}{r} 1\ \ 0\ \ C \\ -\ \ C\ \ 0 \\ \hline 1\ \ C \end{array}.$$

In the tens and hundreds column, $10 - C = 1$ so $C = 9$.
Hence $A = 1, B = 0$ and $C = 9$ which gives

$$\begin{array}{r} 1\ \ 0\ \ 9 \\ -\ \ 9\ \ 0 \\ \hline 1\ \ 9 \end{array}.$$

[An alternative strategy is to convert the problem into an addition. Since $A\,B\,C - C\,B = A\,C$, it follows that

$$\begin{array}{r} A\ \ C \\ +\ \ C\ \ B \\ \hline A\ \ B\ \ C \end{array}.$$

Thus $A = 1$ from the 'carry' and $B = 0$ from the units and $C = 9$ from the tens.]

6. Notice that $1 + 2 + 3 + 4 + 5 + 6 + 7 + 8 = 36$.
To have a units digit of 9 we must reduce the units total by 7,
e.g. $1 + 2 + 3 + 4 + 5 + 6 + 78 = 99$ (7 has been moved into the tens place giving an overall increase of $7 \times 10 - 7 \times 1 = 63$),
or $1 + 23 + 4 + 56 + 7 + 8 = 99$ (2 and 5 become tens so, once again, there is an increase, $(5 + 2) \times 10 - (5 + 2) \times 1 = 63$).

Similarly, starting from $8 + 7 + 6 + 5 + 4 + 3 + 2 + 1 = 36$ and using the same strategy we get $8 + 76 + 5 + 4 + 3 + 2 + 1 = 99$ (7 has been moved from a units position into a tens column), also $8 + 7 + 6 + 54 + 3 + 21 = 99$.
Hence the answer is 'Yes'.

7. Filling the first two rows with eggs gives

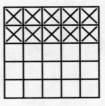

which means that (even if they could be fitted into the columns) 11 eggs cannot work.

Trying to sort out the five in a row, might give

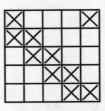

which is fine for rows and columns but contradicts the condition about the diagonal.

But, by moving the eggs down (with a bit of re-cycling) we get this (which is just one of many).

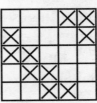

Any egg now placed in this diagram would increase the number of eggs in a row and a column which would give three eggs which is not allowed.

8. (i) It is possible to get 27. For example $4 \times 6 + 3$.

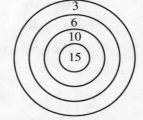

(ii) It is also possible to get 65. The only way with five darts on this board is $3 \times 15 + 2 \times 10$.

(iii) It is not possible to get 59. If a fifteen is not scored, the maximum possible is $5 \times 10 = 50$.
$1 \times 15 = 15$ which would leave 44 in four darts (and $4 \times 10 < 44$).
$2 \times 15 = 30$ which would leave 29 to get with three darts and 2×10 would need 9.
$3 \times 15 = 45$ which would leave 14 to get with two darts.
$4 \times 15 = 60$ which is too big.

9. Label the coins A, B, C, D, E, F and compare A and B with C and D.
(a) If they balance, then the fake is either E or F so weigh these and the fake is the lighter one.
(b) If A and B are lighter than C and D. Then the fake is either A or B so weigh these and the fake is the lighter one.
(c) If C and D are lighter than A and B. Then the fake is either C or D so weigh these and the fake is the lighter one.
    So exactly two weighings are necessary to find the fake.

1998 – 1999 Solutions

1.

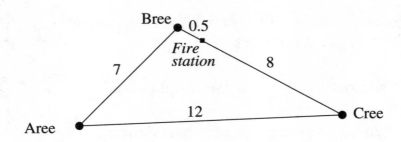

We are told that the greatest distance the fire-engine has to travel to any of the villages is to be as small as it can be. At the position shown in the diagram above, 0.5 km from Bree, the shortest distances to Aree, Bree and Cree are 7.5 km, 0.5 km and 7.5 km respectively. To show that no other position is satisfactory

- At any other position on the road joining Bree to Cree, the shortest distance to either Aree or Cree will be more than 7.5 km.
- At any position on the road joining Aree to Bree, the shortest distance to Cree will be more than 8 km.
- At any position on the road joining Aree to Cree, the shortest distance to either Bree or Cree will be more than 7.5 km.

Hence the fire station should be on the road from Bree to Cree, half a kilometre from Bree.

2. Each person has two neighbours at each meal. Since their neighbours were different at each meal, after three meals each person will have sat next to six different people. This leaves no new people to be neighbours for a fourth meal so the greatest number of meals is three.

To show that it is possible to have had three meals together, a possible seating plan is

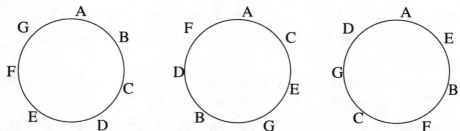

Hence the greatest number of meals they could have had together during the month is three.

3. Emma dusts 100 ornaments in 100 minutes, which is 1 ornament a minute on average. Harry dusts 100 ornaments in 200 minutes, which is half an ornament a minute on average. Thus, working together, they can do 1.5 ornaments a minute on average. 100 ornaments will then take 100 minutes ÷ 1.5 = 66.67 minutes.

It will take them 66.67 minutes if they do it together.

(However, it would probably be better if Harry let Emma complete the last ornament by herself since it might be difficult for them to do it together. Thus Emma dusts 67 ornaments, taking 67 minutes, and Harry dusts 33 ornaments, taking 66 minutes, so the job takes them 67 minutes to complete.)

4. There were 20 boys.
Of the 12 people dressed as ghosts, 9 are boys so 3 are not boys.
There were 5 people not dressed as ghosts and not boys.
Hence the total number at party is 20 + 3 + 5 = 28.

5. The number 1 must not be next to 2 nor 8 next to 7 so each of 1 and 8 can be put next to six numbers.
All other numbers have two numbers which cannot be next to them which means they can be put next to only five numbers.
A number put into either of the two boxes in the middle is next to six numbers so we have to put 1 and 8 in the middle boxes; this determines the positions of 2 and 7. The numbers 3, 4, 5 and 6 can then be placed, noting that 4 and 5 have to be on opposite sides.
One possible solution is:

	7	
3	1	4
5	8	6
	2	

In this solution, the numbers next to 1 are 3, 4, 5, 6, 7, 8; next to 2 are 5, 6, 8; next to 3 are 1, 5, 7, 8; next to 4 are 1, 6, 7, 8; next to 5 are 1, 2, 3, 8; next to 6 are 1, 2, 4, 8; next to 7 are 1, 3, 4; next to 8 are 1, 2, 3, 4, 5, 6.

6. At the end, there were 3 bags of apples.
Add on the half bag sold to the third customer to give half the stock after the second customer. So the stock after the second customer left was $2 \times 3\frac{1}{2} = 7$ bags.
Repeating this – the stock after the first customer left was $2 \times 7\frac{1}{2} = 15$ bags and **the stock at the start was $2 \times 15\frac{1}{2} = 31$ bags.**

7. If the 'added' number is not 1, then the answer will be bigger if we interchange the positions of the added number and 1. For example, the answer for $31 \times 52 + 4$ is 1616, whilst the answer for $34 \times 52 + 1$ is 1769; and the answer for $452 \times 3 + 1$ is 1357.

    When the added number is 1, the numbers in the multiplication use each of 2, 3, 4 and 5 exactly once. There are two cases

    (a) a 3-digit number $\times$ a 1-digit number;

    (b) a 2-digit number $\times$ a 2-digit number.

    For the largest answer, the digits in any 2 or 3 digit number involved are in descending order, reading from left to right. Therefore the multiplication part of the sum is whichever of the following has the biggest value

    Case (a) $543 \times 2 = 1086$; $542 \times 3 = 1626$; $532 \times 4 = 2128$; $432 \times 5 = 2160$.

    Case (b) $54 \times 32 = 1728$; $53 \times 42 = 2226$; $52 \times 43 = 2236$.

    The biggest value for the multiplication is therefore $52 \times 43 = 2236$, and so the biggest possible answer for a calculation as defined in the question is

    $$\mathbf{52 \times 43 + 1 = 2237.}$$

8. If the gardener had not planted any beds on the first day, he would have planted $12 + 24 + 36 + 48 = 120$ in all. In fact, he planted 200.

    Since $200 - 120 = 80$, he planted another $80 \div 5 = 16$ each day.

    Therefore he planted 16 on the first day.

9. If I have only 5p, 2p and 1p coins and cannot make a total of exactly 10p, then the greatest sum of money I can have is 13p (one 5p coin and four 2p coins). Without the 5p coin, the greatest sum would be 9p.

    Similarly, if I have only 50p, 20p and 10p coins and cannot make a total of exactly £1.00, the greatest sum of money that I can have is £1.30 (one 50p coin and four 20p coins). Without the 50p coin, the greatest sum would be 90p. The totals that I can make with one 50p coin and four 20p coins are 20p, 40p, 50p, 60p, 70p, 80p, 90p, £1.10 and £1.30.

    If I also have 5p, 2p and 1p coins in my purse which cannot make an exact total of 10p, I shall still not be able to make exactly £1.00. The greatest possible sum from these extra coins is 13p. Hence if I cannot make the exact £1.00 fare, I can have as much as £1.30 + 13p = £1.43 in my purse. However, there cannot be more than this, and so

    the largest sum of money I could have in my purse is £1.43.

1997 – 1998 Solutions

1. The numbers 1, 2, 3, 4, 5, 6, 7, 8 add up to 36. So, we need numbers for the outer and inner parts each of which total 18 and four pairs of numbers each adding up to 9 for the sectors. The four pairs have to be $1 + 8$, $2 + 7$, $3 + 6$ and $4 + 5$.

   To get the groups of four for the rings notice that if 8 is in a group 1 cannot be, similarly for the others. Also, remember that no duplicates are allowed. Bearing these restrictions in mind, a list can be made as follows:

8	7	2	1	8 & 1
8	6	3	1	8 & 1
8	5	4	1	8 & 1
8	5	3	2	
7	6	4	1	
7	6	3	2	7 & 2
7	5	4	2	7 & 2
6	5	4	3	6 & 3

   So the only sets of numbers are 8, 5, 3, 2 and 7, 6, 4, 1. So one of these is inner and the other outer. One possible solution is shown alongside.

   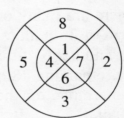

2. Part (i): Yes, for example we could have $83 + 59 + 74 = 216$.

   Part (ii): No, because the sum of three two-digit numbers cannot exceed 297.

3. The total time is 120 minutes for each bike, i.e. 120×6 minutes in total. Therefore each scout must ride for

   $$\frac{120 \times 6}{20} = 36 \text{ minutes.}$$

   One way to do it –

   Ten scouts use three bikes, say A, B, C, for 12 minute periods from 2pm to 4pm as scheduled below:

	Scout									
Times	1	2	3	4	5	6	7	8	9	10
2.00–2.12	A								C	B
2.12–2.24	B	A								C
2.24–2.36	C	B	A							
2.36–2.48		C	B	A						
2.48–3.00			C	B	A					
3.00–3.12				C	B	A				
3.12–3.24					C	B	A			
3.24–3.36						C	B	A		
3.36–3.48							C	B	A	
3.48–4.00								C	B	A

Table 1: Plan A for the scouts

Each of these ten scouts rides for 36 minutes and each bike is in use continuously. The other 10 scouts can use bikes *D, E, F* according to a similar scheme. Replace *A, B, C* by *D, E, F* and scouts 1–10 by scouts 11–20 in the schedule.

There are many other possibilities. One could let 6 scouts ride for their full term of 36 minutes, each using the same bike for the full period. Repeat this for another 6 of the scouts. This leaves 8 scouts, with all 6 bikes available for the remaining 48 minutes. If we divide this into 4 periods of 12 minutes each and arrange for the scouts to ride bikes *A, B, C, D, E, F* we get the following roster:

	Period			
Scout	1	2	3	4
1	A	A	A	
2		B	B	B
3	C		C	C
4	B	C		A
5	D	D	D	
6		E	E	E
7	F		F	F
8	E	F		D

Table 2: Plan B for the scouts

4. In the integers from 1 to 99 there are 20 threes. We can see that by noting that there are 10 threes in the units places: (in 3, 13, 23, 33, 43, 53, 63, 73, 83 and 93) and another 10 in the tens places (in 30, 31, 32, 33, 34, 35, 36, 37, 38, 39).

Similarly there are 20 threes between 100 and 199 and another 20 between 200 and 299. So, up to page 299 we have 60 threes in total.

From 300 to 309 there are 10 + 1 threes, i.e. 11. Similarly there are 11 in 310 to 319 and another 11 in 320 to 329. Thus, by page 329, the total is 60 + 33 = 93 . From then the total goes as follows:

Page:	329	330	331	332	333
Total:	93	95	97	99	102

Thus, since the next page would bring the total to 102,
the number of the last page must be 332.

5. To fill a rectangular area of wall the pins must be arranged in some rectangular pattern. The 36 pins can be arranged as:

(a) 2 rows of 18, (b) 3 rows of 12, (c) 4 rows of 9, or (d) 6 rows of 6.

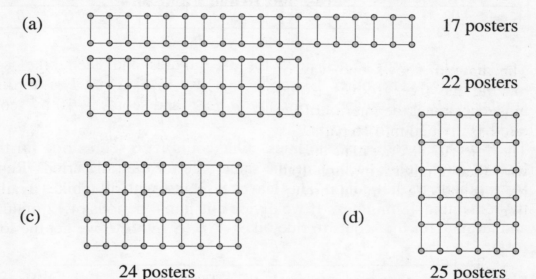

(a)   17 posters

(b)   22 posters

(c)   24 posters

(d)   25 posters

Hence the greatest number of posters that can be pinned up using 36 pins is 25.

6. Draw 'life-lines' to represent ages:

Jock

Wee Jock

Jock has lived for three 'units', compared to Wee Jock's one unit.
Adding a further unit:

Jock

Wee Jock

Jock will be twice as old as Wee Jock at the end of this unit, and so
when Jock is twice as old as Wee Jock,
Wee Jock will be twice as old as he is now.

[Note that there are many possible numerical values which fit the problem but listing them is not going to provide a proof.]

7. Since the third number is the sum of the other two, adding all three together gives twice the third number. Then multiplying by 10 gives 20 times the third number. For this result to equal the product of all three numbers, the product of the first two numbers must be 20. The only pairs of whole numbers whose product is 20 are: 4 and 5, 2 and 10 and 1 and 20.

    The question makes use of 4 and 5.

    For 2 and 10, we have $2 + 10 = 12$ and $2 \times 10 \times 12 = 240$. And, $2 + 10 + 12 = 24$, $24 \times 10 = 240$.

    For 1 and 20, we have $1 + 20 = 21$ then $1 \times 20 \times 21 = 420$ and $1 + 20 + 21 = 42$, $42 \times 10 = 420$.

    The only other pairs of whole numbers with this property are 2 and 10 and 1 and 20.

8. The diagram shows one way of making the five grooves. You must check that the interior of the circle is divided into 16 parts.

    The line *AB* is drawn in such a way that it passes through four regions and *CD* is drawn through five.

    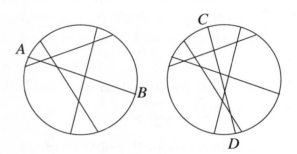

9. Since 13 contestants scored 1 each, the remaining $100 - 13 (= 87)$ contestants scored $289 - 13 (= 276)$ marks. If none of the 87 had scored 4 marks, the total of their marks would have been at most $87 \times 3 (= 261)$. This is 15 short of 276, since $276 - 271 = 15$. It follows that at *least* 15 contestants scored 4 marks each. There could have been exactly 15 with 4 marks, and exactly 72 $(= 87 - 15)$ with 3. The following figures confirm this:

    $15 \times 4 = 60$, $72 \times 3 = 216$, $13 \times 1 = 13$,   and $60 + 216 + 13 = 289$.

    We know that 87 contestants scored at least 2 marks each. Since $87 \times 2 = 174$ and $276 - 174 = 102$, there were 102 marks to bring their totals from 2 to 3 or 4. To bring one mark from 2 to 4 requires an extra 2 marks, and so there were at most $102 \div 2 = 51$ contestants who could have scored 4 marks each. There could have been exactly 51 with 4 marks, together with exactly 36 $(= 87 - 51)$ with 2. The following figures confirm this:

    $51 \times 4 = 204$, $36 \times 2 = 72$, $13 \times 1 = 13$, and $204 + 72 + 13 = 289$.

    Hence:

    the smallest possible number of entrants scoring 4 was 15, and the largest possible number of entrants scoring 4 was 51.

1996 – 1997 Solutions

1. There are lots of possible colourings that work here. For a satisfactory solution you need either to explain a systematic way of doing the colouring, or to demonstrate clearly how your colouring obeys the rules. Here is an example description of a 'systematic' method:

    Developing a systematic method:

    (i)   In any block of 4 squares: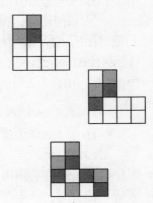

    - Condition (c) means that only one colour is repeated;
    - Condition (a) means that the repeated colour is on diagonally opposite squares.
    - Since the L-shape can be separated into three blocks of four, each of which must contain each colour, condition (b) means that the repeated colour cannot be the same in any two of these three blocks (or we would have more than 4 squares of that colour in total).

    (ii) Start by colouring the first block of 4 in this way:

    then colour the next two squares down so that the new, overlapping, block of four works;

    continue in this way until the whole shape is completed.

    Then check that the result obeys the rules.

Here is an example of how you might write down your colouring check:

Condition (a) : No two squares with an edge in common are the same colour.

Condition (b): There are 4 black, 4 grey and 4 white squares.

Condition (c): There are 5 blocks of 4 squares altogether:

⊞ ⊞ ⊞ ⊞ ⊞ Each of these contains all three colours.

For an extension, you might have looked systematically for all the different possible patterns of colours.

2. Before starting to swap coins in problems like this, it helps to think right through the situation first to see if this gives any extra restrictions. For instance, you might ask yourself, 'What money must everyone be left with after the fares are paid?'

Anne: 14p − 13p = 1p. Hence Anne must have at least one 1p coin.

Boris: 27p − 17p = 10p. Hence Boris must get rid of his 20p coin. He can't use it for his fare as his fare is only 17p, so he must swap it.

Coral: 26p − 22p = 4p. Hence Coral must have two 2p coins, one 2p and two 1p, or four 1p coins.

Damien: 27p − 26p = 1p. Hence Damien must have at least one 1p coin.

Looking at the fares that must be paid:

- Coral and Damien are the only people who can use 20p coins, one each.
- Coral's fare needs two 1p coins or a 2p coin as well as the 20p coin.
- Damien similarly needs either at least one 1p coin or three 2p coins for his fare.
- Anne's fare can be made up only of four 2p coins and a 5p coin or something including at least one 1p coin. So, including her change, she must gain either two 2p coins or two 1p coins.

These restrictions suggest trying the swaps:

- Boris swaps his 20p coin for two 10p coins from Damien.
- Boris swaps his two 1p coins for a 2p coin with Anne.
- Boris swaps his two 2p coins and a 1p coin for a 5p coin with Damien.
- Coral swaps one 5p coin and one 1p coin for three 2p coins with Damien.

Checking that this works:

	20p	10p	5p	2p	1p	Fare required	Change
Anne	0	0	2	1	2	13p	1p
Boris	0	2	1	1	0	17p	10p
Coral	1	0	0	3	0	22p	4p
Damien	1	0	1	0	2	26p	1p

Your solution would not need to show exactly what is here, but would need to show that you had thought about the problem rather than only trying random swaps. (Of course, you might try some random swaps at the start in order to get a feel for the problem, but eventually you would be able to write down some useful thoughts.)

There are alternative solutions: for instance, Anne could swap her two 5ps for a 10p with Boris.

An alternative approach to the solution is for everyone to 'pool' all the coins, and then everyone extracts the coins needed to pay their fare and hold the correct change. You could show this in a table.

3. For problems involving movement or travelling, a diagram often helps you to understand the problem and also to explain it.

	Outward journey	Return journey
Jane	↔	↔
Callum	↔↔↔↔	↔↔

Total distance covered between them is eight times one of Jane's journeys. Since we are told this is 32 miles, then each of Jane's journeys = 4 miles.

Hence Jane travels 8 miles in total.

(*Check*: Callum does 4 × 4 + 2 × 4 = 24 miles, agreeing with the total of 32 miles.)

4. The numbers from 1 to 6 add up to 21.

When the magic number is 10, the total of all three edges is 30 so the corner numbers (which are counted twice) must total 9. The possibilities 1, 2, 6 fails (because we would need 7 in between 1 and 2) as does 2, 3, 4 (as 1 cannot be put with any pair to make 10) but 1, 3, 5 does work, as shown.

When the magic number is 11, the corner numbers must add up to 33 − 21 = 12. Possibilities are: 1, 5, 6 (which fails because 5 + 6 = 11), 2, 4, 6, which works, 3, 4, 5 (which fails as 1 will not work on any side).

When the magic number is 12, the corner numbers must add up to 36 − 21 = 15. The only possibility is 4, 5, 6 which works.

Magic triangles with numbers 10, 11 and 12 can be constructed as follows:

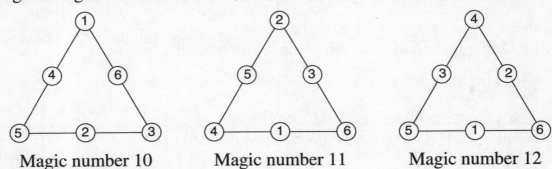

Magic number 10   Magic number 11   Magic number 12

In each case the triangle is magic because the total on each edge is the given magic number.

For an extension, you might show that the only possible magic numbers are 9, 10, 11 and 12: In any magic triangle, the sum of the three edge totals is made up of the sum 1 + 2 + 3 + 4 + 5 + 6 (since each number occurs somewhere) PLUS the three numbers which occur twice i.e. the numbers at the corners. The required smallest magic number is found by placing the three *smallest* numbers at the corners, giving a sum of edge totals of 21 + (1 + 2 + 3) = 27. Since 27 = 3 × 9, there cannot be a magic triangle with number less than 9.

In a similar way, we can work out the largest possible magic triangle number. This occurs when the three largest numbers (i.e. 4, 5 and 6) are placed at the corners, the sum of edge totals being 21 + (4 + 5 + 6) = 36. Dividing this by 3, the number of edges, gives the largest possible number for a magic triangle, i.e. 12.

5. Christmas Carol.
The bird types are shown in *italics* in the question. The following table gives the number of birds sent per day, the number of days sent and the total number of birds of each type sent; summing the last column gives the required total.

type of bird	no. sent/day	no. of days	no. sent
partridge	1	12	12
turtle dove	2	11	22
French hen	3	10	30
colly bird	4	9	36
goose	6	7	42
swan	7	6	42
		Total	184

My true love sent a total of 184 birds over the twelve days of Christmas.
It may be true that in the original carol there were meant to be other references to birds. For instance, many people believe that the 'gold rings' were meant to be *goldfinches* and the 'pipers' *sandpipers*. If you included these items, you would have had to give an explanation of why you were including them and what the common name of the bird was.

6. Morag's Gold Coins.
The answers can be obtained by enumeration:
Numbers which give remainder 1 when divided by 2 are:
$$1, 3, 5, 7, 9, 11, 13, 15, 17, \ldots ;$$
those which give remainder 2 when divided by 3 are:
$$2, 5, 8, 11, 14, 17, 20, 23, 26, \ldots ;$$
those which give remainder 3 when divided by 4 are:
$$3, 7, 11, 15, 19, 23, 27, 31, 35, \ldots .$$
The smallest number occurring in all three of these lists is 11, so
Morag had 11 coins when she was one year old.

In addition, numbers which give remainder 4 when divided by 5 are:
$$4, 9, 14, 19, 24, 29, 34, 39, 44, \ldots .$$
The smallest number occurring in all four lists is 59, so
Morag had 59 coins when she was 12 years old.

Alternatively, you can look for the smallest number which is *one less* than a multiple of 2, *one less* than a multiple of 3 and *one less* than a multiple of 4. This means it is one less than a multiple of 4 × 3 = 12. The smallest such number is 11.

When Morag was 12, her number of coins was also one less than a multiple of 5, so must have been one less than a multiple of 5 × 4 × 3 = 60. The smallest such number is 59.

7. The solid, shown in figure 1, is made up of 7 cubes. The total volume is 189 cubic centimetres, and so each cube has volume 189 ÷ 7 = 27 cubic centimetres.

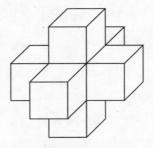 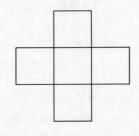

Figure 1   Figure 2

Since all the sides of a cube have the same length, each side has length 3cm. The surface area of the solid is the total area of all the faces on the outside. One cube has no outside faces. Each of the other six cubes has five outside faces, with its net made up of five squares, shown in Figure 2. The area of each net is 5 × 3 × 3 = 45 square centimetres. Therefore

the total surface area of the solid is 6 × 45 = 270 square centimetres.

8. Sarah wants £5 per hour, so altogether she wants to earn £5 × 4 = £20 for herself. Stephen receives 20% of the total payment, and so Sarah receives 80%. Therefore she receives four times as much as Stephen does. It follows that, if she is to receive £20, Stephen will receive £5 and so

the owner must pay £20 + £5 = £25.

9. At the last turn, at most 10 can be added, so you have to force your friend to leave a number of at least 90. You can only do this by leaving your friend a total of exactly 89. You can do this, and stop your friend leaving you with a total of 89 as follows. It makes use of the fact that 89 = 8 × 11 + 1 and that 11 is the sum of the largest and the smallest allowed numbers.

Choose 1 as your first number. Then at each turn if our friend adds on *m* add on (11 − *m*) i.e. whatever your friend adds on, add on that number taken away from 11.

(e.g. if your friend adds on 6, you add on 11 − 6 = 5). This means that, after your first turn, every time your friend and you have both chosen numbers, 11 has been added to the total. In this way, the total after your 9th turn is 89, and you win.

The totals after your moves will be: 1, 12, 23, 34, 45, 56, 67, 78, 89, 100.

1995 – 1996 Solutions

1. From the top two sets of scales, 🧸🧸💣💣🏃🏃 would balance with
🐘🐘💣💣🏃. Removing 💣💣🏃 from both of these collections, we see that
🧸🧸🏃 would be balance with 🐘🐘. It follows that

to balance the third sets of scales we must add 🏃 to the left hand side.

[Alternatively, let t be the weight of a teddy 🧸, let b be the weight of a
balloon 💣, let e be the weight of an elephant 🐘 and let r be the weight of a
runner 🏃. Then $t + 2b = e + r$ and $t + 2r = e + 2b$. Summing these,
we have $2t + 2b + 2r = 2e + 2b + r$ and so, taking $2b + r$ away from
both sides, $2t + r = 2e$. Hence adding a runner to the left hand side of the
third set of scales will balance the right hand side.]

2. By 4.15 p.m., 75 minutes had elapsed since the start. Freddy had then
completed 8 laps (in 72 minutes) and was 3 minutes into his 9th lap.
Therefore he would next cross the line 6 minutes later, at 4.21 p.m. Gerry
had completed 6 laps (in 66 minutes), was 9 minutes into his 7th lap and
would next cross the line 2 minutes later, at 4.17p.m. Harry had completed 9
laps (in 72 minutes), was 3 minutes into his 10th lap and would next cross the
line 5 minutes later, at 4.20 p.m. Hence (by Terry's ruling):

Gerry won the race.

3. We assume that the two planets are going round the star Agg in the same
directions and that the orbits lie in the same plane, as the diagram suggests.
The positions of the planets at the start, after 2 years, after 4 years and after 6
years are as follows:

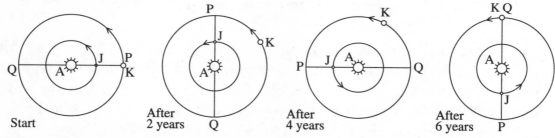

In these diagrams, A, J and K denote the positions of the centres of Agg, Jo
and Ko respectively. A straight line has been drawn joining A and J; this line
meets the orbit of K at points P and Q. At the start, P coincides with K but
then moves ahead of K, whilst Q moves towards K. The points A, J and K will
next be in a straight line when Q catches up with K. This happens when K has
completed ¼ of its orbit, which is after six years, as shown. Therefore

Agg, Jo and Ko will next be in a straight line six years from now.

*Note: the question does not say that the three objects have to be in line in the
same order. They will be in line in the same order after 12 years.*

4. In the question, we are given that $132 = 13 + 12 + 21 + 23 + 31 + 32$. Multiply each digit in this by 2; this gives $264 = 26 + 24 + 42 + 46 + 62 + 64$ and so 264 is another 3-digit number which satisfies the required properties. Similarly, multiplying each digit in the expression for 132 by 3, we get $396 = 39 + 36 + 63 + 69 + 93 + 96$. However, multiplying each digit by 4 is no use for our purposes, because $3 \times 4 = 12$, which has two digits.

In general, we should consider any 3-digit number with its digits all different. The sum of the six 2-digit numbers which can be formed from the three digits can be turned into a sum of twelve numbers by separating each 2-digit number as $10 \times$ the first digit plus the second digit. For example, for 358 the sum is $35 + 38 + 53 + 58 + 83 + 85$, which is equal to

$$(3 \times 10 + 5) + (3 \times 10 + 8) + (5 \times 10 + 3) + (5 \times 10 + 8) + (8 \times 10 + 3) + (8 \times 10 + 5).$$

For any 3-digit number, abc ($= 100a + 10b + c$), this sum is

$$(10a + b) + (10a + c) + (10b + a) + (10b + c) + (10c + a) + (10c + b)$$

$$= 22a + 22b + 22c.$$

This expression tells us that the original number is a multiple of 22.

The following table lists the possible 3-digit multiples of 22. We use it to find every 3-digit number (with digits all different) which is equal to the sum of its digits $\times$ 22. As 9 is the biggest digit and the digits are all different, the sum of the digits of the 3-digit number cannot be greater than $9 + 8 + 7 = 24$. Thus the table need go only as far as 24.

(a) Multiple of 22	(b) Sum of digits	(c) Sum of digits × 22	Is (a) =(c)?
$6 \times 22 = 132$	6	132	Yes (Already known)
$7 \times 22 = 154$	10	220	No
$8 \times 22 = 176$	14	308	No
$9 \times 22 = 198$	18	396	No
$12 \times 22 = 264$	12	264	Yes
$13 \times 22 = 286$	16	352	No
$14 \times 22 = 308$	11	242	No
$16 \times 22 = 352$	10	220	No
$17 \times 22 = 374$	14	308	No
$18 \times 22 = 396$	18	396	Yes
$19 \times 22 = 418$	13	286	No
$21 \times 22 = 462$	12	264	No
$23 \times 22 = 506$	11	242	No
$24 \times 22 = 528$	15	330	No

Note: numbers such as $10 \times 22 = 220$ and $11 \times 22 = 242$ are omitted, since two digits are the same.

Thus:

264 and 396 are the only other 3-digit numbers which satisfy the required properties.

An alternative to the table above is consider the equation below which comes from knowing the the number is equal to the sum of the six 2-digit numbers formed from it.

$$100a + 10b + c = 22a + 22b + 22c.$$

By subtracting an a and a b and a c from each side we get

$$99a + 9b = 21a + 21b + 21c$$

which, on dividing by 3, becomes

$$33a + 3b = 7a + 7b + 7c$$

or $\quad 3(11a + b) = 7(a + b + c).$

From this we can say that $a + b + c$ is a multiple of 3 and also that $11a + b$ is a multiple of 7. This leads to a smaller table

a	$11a$	$11a + b$	b	Possible numbers
1	11	14	3	132; 135; 138
2	22	28	6	261; 264; 267
3	33	35	2	321; 324; 327
3	33	42	9	393; 396; 399
4	44	49	5	453; 456; 459
5	55	56	1	513; 516; 519
5	55	63	8	582; 585; 588
6	66	70	4	642; 645; 648
7	77	84	7	771; 774; 777
8	88	91	3	831; 834; 837
9	99	105	6	963; 966; 969

From the 'possible numbers' we have to reject those which repeat any digits and odd numbers (since they have to be divisible by 22 and hence by 2). This gives 132; 138; 264; 324; 396; 456; 516; 582; 642; 648 and 834. The only ones in this list which are multiples of 22 are: 132, 264 and 396.

5. On the second day, exactly $\frac{3}{4}$ of the total membership took part and so the total number of members was exactly divisible by 4. For every 4 members, 3 took part on the second day and 2 on the third day, so the numbers of miles covered on the three days by a group of 4 members would have been:

$$4 \times 18 + 3 \times 13 + 2 \times 9 = 72 + 39 + 18 = 129.$$

Since the total number of miles covered was between 1000 and 1100 we need a number between these which is a multiple of 129. Since $1100 \div 129 = 8\frac{68}{129}$, we can deduce that the total number of miles is $8 \times 129 = 1032$.

the exact figure was 1032, and there were $8 \times 4 = $ 32 members last year.

6. The ten palindromic perfect squares less than 100000 are

121   484   676   10201   12321   14641   40804   44944   69696   94249,

which are

11^2 22^2 26^2 101^2 111^2 121^2 202^2 212^2 264^2 307^2

respectively. To find these numbers, we can find the squares of all positive integers in turn until we reach 317^2, which equals 100489 and so has 6 digits. There is no need to go any further, because all subsequent squares will have 6 or more digits. The work can be reduced if we use the fact that squares of integers must end in one of 0, 1, 4, 5, 6 or 9, so that palindromic squares cannot start with 2, 3, 7 or 8. Thus we do not need to look at squares between 20000 and 39999, or between 70000 and 89999.

There is only one digit missing in the list of palindromic squares, the digit 5. The different letters used in the coded forms are D, A, O, E, R, M, L, N and P. What word involves these letters and one other? There is a word in the statement of the question which fulfils these requirements: PALINDROME. In this, the extra letter is I and it corresponds to the missing digit. Therefore, for this word

the letter which is not used is I and its value is 5.

[Notes.
1. Any sensible alternative for the word is acceptable.
2. To answer the question, it is not necessary to decode the expressions for the palindromic squares. However, this can be done as follows: the squares are

    121   484   676   10201   12321   14641   40804   44944   69696   94249,

    and their coded versions are

    DAD DAOAD DEAED DRMRD LRARL MLMLM MNM REPER RPR RRLRR.

    Count the numbers of times that the different digits occur and the different letters occur. We find that 1 is the only digit, and D the only letter, occurring 8 times. Hence D = 1. Similarly, 4 is the only digit, and R the only letter, occurring 12 times. Hence R = 4. Then A = 2, because DAD can only be 121, and similarly O = 3, E = 0 (take care to distinguish between the letter O and the figure 0), M = 6, P = 8, L = 9 and N = 7.]

2000 – 2001 Junior Solutions

1. In a quarter of an hour, the faster train will travel 20 miles and the slower train will travel 15 miles. Adding these distances shows that

   the trains are 35 miles apart.

   [An alternative argument is to observe that the speed at which the two trains approach each other is 140 mph. Thus in a quarter of an hour this amounts to $140 \div 4 = 35$ miles. Thus a quarter of an hour before they pass they are 35 miles apart.]

2. If all members had paid their subscriptions and the extra £2.99, the total collected would have been £401.99 = 40,199 pence. Thus 40,199 must be divisible by the number of members (which is less than 100). Now 40,199 = 61×659 and these factors, 61 and 659, are both prime. The only one of these factors which is less than 100 is 61. (1 is not possible as there are at least two members.) Thus the club had 61 members and each paid 659 pence = £6.59. So the subscription was £6.59 – £2.99 = £3.60.

   There were 61 members and the annual subscription was £3.60.

3. The prime numbers less than 100 are 2, 3, 5, 7, 11, 13, 17, 19, 23, 29, 31, 37, 41, 43, 47, 53, 59, 61, 67, 71, 73, 79, 83, 89, 97.

   Consider adding together the two diagonals and the middle row, this total is 3×111. In such a sum, each of the numbers in the two outside columns appears exactly once, adding up to 2×111, and the middle entry occurs three times. So the middle entry is one third of 111 i.e. 37, and so the bottom middle entry is 73. Now, the bottom left entry must be a prime number, p say, such that, from the diagonal, $74 - p$, is prime. The only pairs of primes which total 74 are (3, 71), (7, 67), (13, 61), (31, 43) and (37, 37).

   In the bottom row, $38 - p$ is prime and (7, 31) and (19, 19) are the only pairs of primes which total 38. Since p has to be in both this list and the one above, $p = 7$. This gives

	1	67
	37	
7	73	31

   and the rest is straightforward, giving

43	1	67
61	37	13
7	73	31

   .

4. Since every fourth power is also a square, it is sufficient to obtain the smallest integer greater than 1 which is a cube and a fourth power.

   Since 3 and 4 have no common factors, any number that is a cube and a fourth power must be a 12th power. Thus, raising the smallest allowed number to this power, the required number is 2^{12} and so

   the smallest integer greater than 1 which is a square,
   a cube and a fourth power is 4096.

5. From the first and last parts of the equation, M + # + ✪ = # + M + # + #
    we can deduce that ✪ = # + #.
    Putting this into the first and middle parts, we get
         M + # + # + # = # + # + # + # + # + # + # + #
    giving   M = # + # + # + # + #.
    So, because M = 5, we can say that # = **1 and ✪ = 2.**

6. The solution to this problem does not depend on the starting points so, for
    convenience, assume that the Sun, Venus and Earth are in line. Consider the
    ratio of the times of the orbits as given below

    $$\frac{\text{Earth orbit}}{\text{Venus orbit}} = \frac{365.2564}{224.643} \approx 1.6259$$

    which means that in the time the Earth takes to complete one orbit, Venus
    completes 1.6259 orbits. We need to find a whole numbers N and M so that
    when the Earth has completed N orbits, Venus has completed M orbits (to
    within two days). For N orbits, the Earth takes $365.2564N$ days and for M
    orbits, Venus takes $224.643M$ days. So these numbers must be within x days
    of each other, where x is less than 2. So $x + 365.2564N = 224.643M$.
    Dividing by 224.643 gives

    $$M = \frac{365.2564}{224.643}N + \frac{x}{224.643}.$$

    Now, $\frac{365.2564}{224.643}$ is equal to 1.626 and $\frac{x}{224.643}$ is less than 0.01. So $1.626N$ is
    within 0.01 of M. The first multiple of 1.626 which is sufficiently close to a
    whole number is 8 and this multiple is close to 13. Finally we check that 8
    Earth orbits take $8 \times 365.2564 = 2922.0512$ days and 13 Venus orbits take
    $13 \times 224.643 = 2920.359$ days. Thus, both Earth and Venus will have
    completed a whole number of orbits

    in about 2921 days.

7. The total of the volumes of the flasks, 12 + 15 + 27 + 35 + 37 + 40 + 53 + 69,
    is 288. So that the volumes of the flasks which are filled can be divided in
    the ratio 1 : $1\frac{1}{2}$, their total must be divisible by $2\frac{1}{2}$. But, we are dealing with
    whole numbers and that means the total is only divisible by $2\frac{1}{2}$ if it is divisible
    by 5. Since when 288 is divided by 5 there is a remainder of 3, the volume of
    the empty flask must also leave a remainder of 3 when it is divided by 5. The
    volume of the only flask for which this is true is 53.

    We now require a set of flasks (excluding 53) which total $\frac{2}{5} \times 235 = 94$.
    Subtracting the higher values in turn gives

94 − 69 = 25	not possible
94 − 40 = 54 = 27 + 15 + 12	possible
94 − 37 = 57	not possible.

So, the empty flask held 53 fluid ounces, the flasks 40, 27, 15, 12 held water and the flasks 69, 37, 35 held alcohol.

[It is possible to use algebra to establish the volume of the empty flask.

Let the volume of water used be V_W, the volume of alcohol used be V_A and the empty flask have volume V_E. Then we are given that $V_A = 1\frac{1}{2}V_W$ and that the total capacity of all the flasks is $12 + 15 + 27 + 35 + 37 + 40 + 53 + 69 = 288$. Thus

$$V_A + V_W + V_E = 288$$

$$\text{so } 2\frac{1}{2}V_W + V_E = 288.$$

But V_E is a whole number so when it is subtracted from 288 a whole number results into which $2\frac{1}{2}$ must divide exactly. The only whole numbers into which $2\frac{1}{2}$ divides exactly are ones which are multiples of 5. The outcome of this is that the units digit of V_E must be either 3 or 8 and so $V_E = 53$ and $2\frac{1}{2}V_W = 235$ giving $V_W = 94$.]

8. The prime numbers between 10 and 100 are

11	13	17	19	23	29	31	37	41	43	47
53	59	61	67	71	73	79	83	89	97	

Condition (i) eliminates 11, 13, 17, 19, 23, 31, 37, 41, 43, 53, 59, 61, 71, 73, 79, 97, leaving

29	47	67	83	89

The sum of these five primes is 315 which is not prime ($315 = 5 \times 63$) so the collection contains fewer than five primes.

Since each of these primes is odd, any set of four will add up to give an even number so that the collection cannot contain four primes.

The same argument applies to any pair of these numbers so that the original collection contained three primes. So we now list the possible triples, their sum and, where relevant, the digit sum of the sum.

Numbers	Sum	Digit sum	Numbers	Sum	Digit sum
29, 47, 67	$143 = 13 \times 11$		29, 83, 89	$201 = 3 \times 67$	
29, 47, 83	$159 = 3 \times 53$		47, 67, 83	197	17
29, 47, 89	$165 = 3 \times 5 \times 11$		47, 67, 89	$203 = 7 \times 29$	
29, 67, 83	179	17	47, 83, 89	$219 = 3 \times 73$	
29, 67, 89	$185 = 5 \times 37$		67, 83, 89	239	14

As the table shows, there are only three triples whose sum is prime and two of these give a final prime. So the original primes are either 29, 67 and 83 or 47, 67 and 83. Thus the third prime could be 29 or 47 but

two of the original prime numbers are 67 and 83.

1999 – 2000 Junior Solutions

1. The total number of votes cast was 58335 and 4 candidates took part.
   Suppose that the winner polled V votes.
   The three rivals then polled $V - 569$, $V - 1772$ and $V - 2880$ votes.
   Totalling all the votes cast gives

   $$V + (V - 569) + (V - 1772) + (V - 2880) = 58335$$

   $$\text{so} \qquad 4V = 63556$$

   $$\text{giving} \qquad V = 15889.$$

   The votes received by the 4 candidates
   were 15889, 15320, 14117, 13009.

2. Consider the time taken by the pensioner and a bus to travel the 2 km
   between home and the shop. Using the formula $\text{Time} = \dfrac{\text{Distance}}{\text{Speed}}$:–

Pensioner	$T = \frac{2}{5}$ hour $= 24$ minutes	
Bus	$T = \frac{2}{45}$ hour $= \frac{8}{3}$ minutes $= 2$ min 40 secs	

   The bus and the pensioner meet halfway between his home and the shop, so
   they meet at 08:12 on a day when he sets off at 08:00.
   There are two cases to consider depending on which way the bus is travelling.

   (a) Buses going in the same direction as the pensioner:
   The bus which passes the pensioner at 08:12 will reach the shop 1 min
   20 secs later, i.e. at 08:13:20. It is a 30 minute service, so buses will
   arrive at the shop as follows:

         07:13:20   07:43:20   08:13:20

   The buses must have passed his home 2 mins 40 secs prior to these
   times, i.e. at

         07:10:40   07:40:40   08:10:40

   (b) Buses going in the opposite direction to the pensioner:
   These buses would leave the shop at 07:13:20; 07:43:20 and 08:13:20
   and would arrive at his home 2 mins 40 secs later, as follows:

         07:16   07:46   08:16

   A distance-time graph *may* be usefully used to relate all these ideas.

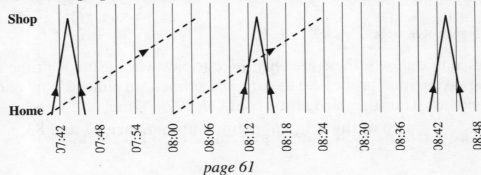

On the day when the pensioner leaves home at 07:40 we can list the movements as follows:

	Home		Half way		Shop
Pensioner	07:40	→	07:52	→	08:04
Bus 1	07:10:40	→	07:12	→	07:13:20 – too early
Bus 2	07:40:40	→	07:42	→	07:43:20
Bus 3	08:10:40	→	08:12	→	08:13:20 – too late
Bus 4	07:16	←	07:14:40	←	07:13:20 – too early
Bus 5	07:46	←	07:44:40	←	07:43:20
Bus 6	08:16	←	08:14:40	←	08:13:20 – too late

From the table it is clear that only two buses would pass the pensioner

Bus 2 passing his home at 07:40:40

and　　　　Bus 5 passing the shop at 07:43:20.

For Bus 2, the pensioner leaves home at 07:40 and the bus passes his home 40 seconds later. In this 40 seconds, the distance walked by the pensioner is $\frac{40}{60} \times \frac{1}{12}$ km = $\frac{1}{18}$ km. So, the bus has to catch up with the pensioner. The difference in their speeds is 40 km/hr. At this rate, the time taken for the bus to pass the pensioner is $\frac{1}{18} \div \frac{2}{3} = \frac{1}{12}$ min = 5 sec. The distance covered by the bus in 5 seconds is $\frac{1}{12} \times \frac{3}{4} = \frac{1}{16}$ km. So the pensioner must have been $\frac{1}{16}$ km from home when the bus passed him travelling in the same direction.

For Bus 5, at 07:43:20 the pensioner has now been walking for 200 seconds. His distance from home can be calculated easily by observing that in 40 seconds he walks $\frac{1}{18}$ km. So he is $\frac{5}{18}$ km from home which is $\frac{31}{18}$ km from the shop. The bus and pensioner are approaching at a speed of 50 km/hr. At this speed, the time taken to cover $\frac{31}{18}$ km is $\frac{31}{18} \div 50$ hr = $\frac{31}{900} \times 60$ min = $\frac{31}{15} \times 60$ sec, i.e. 124 seconds. In this time, the distance walked by the pensioner is $\frac{124}{60} \times \frac{1}{12}$ km = $\frac{31}{180}$ km so his distance from home is then $\frac{5}{18} + \frac{31}{180} = \frac{81}{180}$ km = $\frac{9}{20}$ km.

The pensioner is passed by a bus going in the same direction $\frac{1}{16}$ km from home and by a second bus going in the opposite direction $\frac{9}{20}$ km from home.

3.　The hour hand moves 30° in 1 hour which is $\frac{1}{2}$ degree in one minute. The minute hand moves 6° in 1 minute.

At 5 minutes to 2, $\angle AOO' = 30°$.

The hour hand is $5 \times \frac{1}{2}°$ before the '2' position so

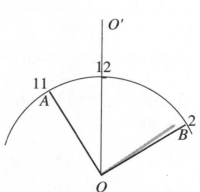

$$\angle O'OB = \left(60 - 2\tfrac{1}{2}\right)° = 57\tfrac{1}{2}°$$

The angle between the hands at 5 minutes to 2 o'clock is $87\tfrac{1}{2}°$.

Now, to find when the angle between the hands is 90°:

The minute hand moves 6° each minute.

The hour hand moves $\frac{1}{2}$° each minute.

So the minute hand moves $5\frac{1}{2}$° further than the hour hand each minute.

Initially, the hands are getting closer together so the minute hand must pass the hour hand before the angle between them can reach 90°. Since

$$87\frac{1}{2} \div 5\frac{1}{2} = \frac{175}{2} \div \frac{11}{2} = \frac{175}{11}$$

it takes $\frac{175}{11}$ minutes for the two hands to meet.

For the next 90°,

$$90 \div 5\frac{1}{2} = 90 \div \frac{11}{2} = \frac{180}{11}$$

so it takes a further $\frac{180}{11}$ mins for the angle between the hands to reach 90°.

It takes a total of $\frac{355}{11} = 32\frac{3}{11}$ minutes until the hands make an angle of 90°.

[An algebraic solution to the second part could be:

As the angle between the hands just after 5 minutes to 2 is decreasing, the next time the hands will be at 90° will be shortly before half past 2. We determine exactly when as follows: Suppose it occurs at x minutes past 2. In every minute, the hour hand moves $\frac{1}{2}$° and the minute hand moves 6°. So, at x minutes past 2, the hands will be at right angles if $6x - \left(60 + \frac{1}{2}x\right) = 90$. Solving this gives $x = 27\frac{3}{11}$ minutes. Thus the time elapsing is $32\frac{3}{11}$ minutes.]

4. Since there are 8 rows and no more than 2 eggs per row, no more than 16 eggs can be placed in the box. It is possible to 16 eggs in the box satisfying the conditions given. This can be done in many ways and we give one systematic way to go about achieving this.

Starting with 2 eggs in each column, placed in the first two rows gives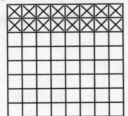

Trying to sort out the eight in a row, might give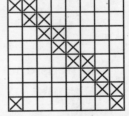

which is fine for rows and columns but contradicts the condition about the diagonal.

By moving the eggs down (with a bit of re-cycling) we get this.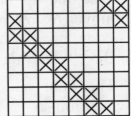

Any egg now placed in this diagram would increase the number of eggs in a row and a column which would give three eggs which is not allowed.

5. Suppose that the head of mathematics thought that there were x good students. Then the rector thought that there were $\frac{3}{2}x$, the youngest teacher thought that there were

$$\tfrac{3}{2}x + \tfrac{1}{3} \times \tfrac{3}{2}x = 2x$$

and the oldest teacher thought that there were

$$\tfrac{1}{3} \times 2x = \tfrac{2}{3}x.$$

Since this differs from the head of department's figure by 12,

$$x - \tfrac{2}{3}x = 12$$
$$\text{so} \qquad x = 36.$$

The head of department thought that there were 36 good mathematical students.

6. The number lies between 1234000 and 1234999.
Using a calculator, $\sqrt{1234000} \approx 1110{\cdot}85$ and $\sqrt{1234999} \approx 1111{\cdot}30$.
Only one integer lies between $1110{\cdot}85$ and $1111{\cdot}30$, namely 1111.
Now $1111^2 = 1234321$ so **the square root of the number is 1111**.

7. There are 25 coins, one lighter than the others. Divide the coins into three piles, containing 8, 8 and 9 coins.
   Weighing 1 Compare the weights of the 2 piles of 8 coins. If they balance, the counterfeit coin is in the pile of 9. If they do not balance, the odd coin is in the light pile of 8.
   Weighing 2 Divide the pile containing the counterfeit into either three piles of 3 coins or two piles of 3 coins and a pile of 2 coins.
   Compare the weights of two piles of 3 coins and this will indicate the pile of either 2 or 3 coins containing the counterfeit.
   Weighing 3 If only 2 coins are left, weigh them.
   If 3 coins are left, compare any 2 of the 3 and this will indicate the counterfeit.

The smallest number of coins in which a counterfeit coin can be detected by a single weighing is three. So the smallest number of coins in which a counterfeit coin can be detected by two weighing is 9. So we need at least three weighings for 25 coins and we have achieved this.

Thus only three weighings are required.

1998 – 1999 Junior Solutions

1. For the first digit of the 4-digit number there are four choices. For each of these four choices, there are three choices for the second digit, two choices for the third digit and the last digit is then fixed.

Thus there are 4 × 3 × 2 × 1 = 24 different 4-digit numbers.

A complete list of these is

7531	7513	7351	7315	7153	7135
5731	5713	5371	5317	5173	5137
3751	3715	3571	3517	3175	3157
1753	1735	1573	1537	1375	1357

In the thousands place, a quarter of these (i.e. 6) have 1, a quarter have 3, a quarter have 5 and a quarter have 7. Thus the sum of the thousands digits of all 24 numbers is $6 \times (1 + 3 + 5 + 7) \times 1000 = 96000$. Similarly, a quarter of the numbers have 1 in the hundreds position, a quarter have 3, a quarter have 5 and a quarter have 7, so the sum of the hundreds digits is $6 \times (1 + 3 + 5 + 7) \times 100 = 9600$. In a similar way the sum of the tens digits of all 24 numbers is 960 and the sum of the units digits is 96. Thus the sum of all 24 numbers is

$6 \times (1 + 3 + 5 + 7) \times 1111 = 96000 + 9600 + 960 + 96 = 106\,656.$

If a digit can be used more than once, there are $4 \times 4 \times 4 \times 4$ different numbers since there are 4 choices for each digit. Thus there are $4^4 = 256$ different 4-digit numbers. One quarter of 256 is 64 so, using a similar argument to that above, the sum of all 256 numbers will be

$64 \times (1 + 3 + 5 + 7) \times (1000 + 100 + 10 + 1) = 1\,137\,664.$

2. In the time that Catriona ran 100 metres, Morag ran 80 metres so they are level but both have 20 metres to go to reach the finish line. Dividing 100 and 80 by 5, we can see that whilst Catriona ran the last 20 metres, Morag ran 16 metres.

So Catriona arrived first with Morag 4 metres behind.

[Alternative: Morag ran 80 metres in the time that Catriona ran 100 metres so Morag runs at 4/5 the speed of Catriona. Every race they run, Morag will run only 4/5 of the distance that Catriona runs in the same time. While Catriona runs 120 metres, Morag will run 4/5 of 120 metres = 96 metres.]

3. There are two acceptable answers. If captives can be left alone on one side or on the boat, the answer is 'yes'. The following scheme shows one possible way that all six people can be transferred, denoting each soldier by S, each captive by C and the captive who can row by C*.

Step	Side 1	Over	Back	Side 2
0	SSS C*CC	C*C	C*	C
1	SSS C*C	C*C	C*	CC
2	SSS C*	SS	S C	S C
3	SS C*C	S C*	S C	S C*
4	SS CC	SS	C*	SSS
5	C*CC	C*C	C*	SSS C
6	C*C	C*C	–	SSS C*CC

If the requirement that there must be more soldiers than captives is taken as excluding the possibility of captives being left alone on one side, the answer is 'no'. The reason is that, in the first crossing, if two captives cross, no one can be left on the second side; if a captive and a soldier cross and the captive rows back, on his landing there would be three captives and two soldiers on one side; two soldiers cannot cross since this would leave three captives and only one soldier on the first side.

4. The two-digit prime numbers are
11, 13, 17, 19, 23, 29, 31, 37, 41, 43, 47, 53, 59, 61, 67, 71, 73, 79, 83, 89, 97.
Looking for pairs which add and subtract to give two-digit numbers using different digits, as required, gives the following possibilities

	Primes	Sum	Difference
(i)	13 and 59	72	46
(ii)	13 and 67	80	54
(iii)	37 and 61	98	24

In (i) and (iii), one of the remaining unused digits is 0 so only
13 and 67 can be the house numbers with the third house being number 29.

5.   We know that A + B = 99, that A is a multiple of 4 and that B is a multiple of 7. Since A is positive, B is less than 99. The possible values of B are therefore 7, 14, 21, 28, 35, 42, 49, 56, 63, 70, 77, 84, 91 and 98. Of these, each of 21, 42, 63 and 84 is 7 times the sum of its digits. The corresponding values of A, given by A + B = 99, are 78, 57, 36 and 15, of which only 36 is a multiple of 4. We can verify that 36 is 4 times the sum of the digits, and
so the required values are given by A = 36 and B = 63.
[Alternative: Let A = $10a + b$ and B = $10c + d$. We are told that

$$10a + b = 4(a + b) \Rightarrow 6a = 3b \Rightarrow b = 2a,$$

$$\text{and } 10c + d = 7(c + d) \Rightarrow 3c = 6d \Rightarrow c = 2d.$$

But A + B = 99, so $10a + 10c + b + d = 99$. However, the final 9 means that $b + d = 9$ as the biggest total of two single digits is 18. Thus $a + c = 9$ as well. Using $b = 2a$ and $c = 2d$, these become

$$2a + d = 9 \text{ or } a = 9 - a - d$$

$$a + 2d = 9 \text{ or } d = 9 - a - d.$$

So $a = d$ and both are 3 giving $b = c = 6$.]

6.   The answer is 'No'.
The square of an even positive integer is always even, and so the final digit is even.
For the odd positive integers, the final digit of the square is odd, but for squares greater than 10, the tens digit is always even.

Proof.
The last two digits of the squares of the odd integers 5, 7, 9, 11, 13, 15, 17, 19, 21, 23 and 25 are 25, 49, 81, 21, 69, 25, 89, 61, 41, 29 and 25 respectively.
The last two digits of the squares of the odd integers from 25 to 49 are these same numbers but in reverse order, with 09 and 01 added:
25, 29, 41, 61, 89, 25, 69, 21, 81, 49, 25, 09, and 01.
The squares of the odd integers from 51 to 99 inclusive, end with the digits:
01, 09, 25, 49, 81, 21, 69, 25, 89, 61, 41, 29, 25, 29, 41, 61, 89, 25, 69, 21, 81, 49, 25, 09, 01 and for the squares of the subsequent odd integers, the same pattern is repeated indefinitely. Hence for squares greater than 10, the tens digit is always even.

[Alternatively, we can express any odd integer n greater than 10 in the form $10x + y$, where x is a positive integer and y is one of 1, 3, 5, 7 and 9. Then $n^2 = 100x^2 + 20xy + y^2$, and y^2 is one of 1, 9, 25, 49 and 81, none of which have an odd number of tens. Since $n^2 = 100x^2 + 20xy + y^2$, the tens digit comes from $2xy$ (plus any carry from y^2). Thus, because $2xy$ is even and so is any carry, the tens digit of n^2 is therefore even.]

1997 – 1998 Junior Solutions

1.

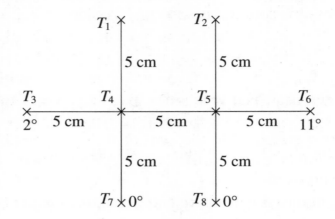

Since the temperature at any point on the wire is halfway between the temperatures at any two points the same distance away on either side, the temperature increases uniformly along the wire. So, over the three sections from T_3 to T_6 there is an increase of 9°, so each segment must increase by 3°, giving $T_4 = 5°$ and $T_5 = 8°$. Since T_4 is halfway between T_7 and T_1, the latter is 10°. Similar reasoning gives $T_2 = 16°$. So

$$T_1 = 10°, \qquad T_2 = 16°, \qquad T_4 = 5°, \qquad T_5 = 8°.$$

[Using algebra, we can say: $T_4 = (T_1 + T_7)/2$, so $T_1 = 2T_4$ and similarly $T_2 = 2T_5$. Also, $T_4 = (T_3 + T_5)/2 = 1 + T_5/2$; $T_5 = (T_4 + T_6)/2 = 11/2 + T_4/2 = 11/2 + (1 + T_5//2)/2 = 6 + T_5/4$. So $T_5 = 8$ and the rest follow.]

2. The numbers 1, 2, 3, 4, 5, 6, 7, 8 add up to 36. So, we need numbers for the outer and inner parts each of which total 18 and four pairs of numbers each adding up to 9 for the sectors. The four pairs have to be $1 + 8$, $2 + 7$, $3 + 6$ and $4 + 5$.

To get the groups of four for the rings notice that if 8 is in a group 1 cannot be, similarly for the others. Also, remember that no duplicates are allowed. Bearing these restrictions in mind, a list can be made as follows:

8	7	2	1	8 & 1
8	6	3	1	8 & 1
8	6	2	2	2 & 2
8	5	4	1	8 & 1
8	5	3	2	
8	4	3	3	3 & 3
7	6	4	1	
7	6	3	2	7 & 2
7	5	4	2	7 & 2
7	5	3	3	3 & 3
7	4	3	2	7 & 2
6	5	4	3	6 & 3

So the only sets of numbers are 8, 5, 3, 2 and 7, 6, 4, 1. So one of these is inner and the other outer. One possible solution is shown alongside.

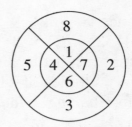

When the larger circle is divided into five, there are 10 zones. The sum of all ten numbers $1 + 2 + 3 + 3 + 4 + 5 + 6 + 7 + 8 + 9 + 10 = 55$. If the sum of the inner numbers were equal to the sum of the outer numbers then each would be a whole number equal to half of 55. However 55 is *odd*, so half of it cannot be a whole number.

Therefore the numbers **cannot** be entered in the manner described.

3. The difference between the two weights, $740 - 560 = 180$ grams, is the weight of three fifths of a jugful of water. Hence one fifth of a jugful weighs 60 grams. Since the weight of the jug plus one fifth of a jugful weighs 560 grams,

    the jug itself must weigh 500 grams.

4. Trial and improvement method.
    Try 10 children: Meg would then have 10 children, 10×9 grandchildren, $10 \times 9 \times 8$ great-grandchildren giving 820 descendants – too many.

    Hence, she has fewer than 10 children, but we can speed the process by checking only the biggest number, that of the great-grandchildren.

    $9 \times 8 \times 7 = 504$ too big; $8 \times 7 \times 6 = 336$ too big; $7 \times 6 \times 5 = 210$ possible.

    Try 7 children: This gives 7×6 grandchildren and 210 great-grandchildren so 259 descendants in total – the required number.

    However, we need to check that there are no other solutions.

    Try 6 children: This gives $6 \times 5 \times 4 = 120$ great-grandchildren, $6 \times 5 = 30$ grandchildren and 6 children – a total of 156 descendants which is too few.

    Since a smaller number of children will give a smaller total, we can conclude that

    Meg has 7 daughters.

    [Alternatively, let Meg have n daughters. So each daughter had $(n - 1)$ daughters and each granddaughter had $(n - 2)$ daughters. So the total of Meg's descendents is

    $$n + n(n - 1) + n(n - 1)(n - 2) = 259.$$

    But n appears in each term on the left and since $259 = 7 \times 37$ and both 7 and 37 are prime n must be 7 or 37. The value of 37 produces a massive 47989 descendents and, as we know, this means Meg had 7 daughters.]

5. Since $8 = 2^3$, $9 = 3^2$ and $891 = 81 \times 11 = 3^4 \times 11$ we can say that $64152 = 2^3 \times 3^6 \times 11$. Since 11 is a prime number, the required 3-digit number must be a multiple of 11. We find all 3-digit factors of 64152 which are multiples of 11, starting with those which do not have 2 as a factor, then those having 2, then 2^2, then 2^3 as a factor. These numbers are

$3^3 \times 11 = 297$,	$3^4 \times 11 = 891$,	$2 \times 3^2 \times 11 = 198$,
$2 \times 3^3 \times 11 = 594$,	$2^2 \times 3 \times 11 = 132$,	$2^2 \times 3^2 \times 11 = 396$,
$2^3 \times 3 \times 11 = 264$,	$2^3 \times 3^2 \times 11 = 792$.	

Thus the 3-digit number is one of 297, 891, 198, 594, 132, 396, 264 and 792. Since 64152 does not have 7 as a factor, we can rule out 297 and 792. Similarly 64152 does not have 5 as a factor, so we can rule out 594. That leaves 891, 198, 132, 396 and 264. We know from the question that $8 \times 9 \times 1 \times 891 = 64152$. For the remaining numbers:

$1 \times 9 \times 8 \times 198 = 14256$,	$1 \times 3 \times 2 \times 132 = 792$,
$\mathbf{3 \times 9 \times 6 \times 396 = 64152}$ and	$2 \times 6 \times 4 \times 264 = 12672$.

It follows that

another way of expressing 64152 in the required form is
$3 \times 9 \times 6 \times 396 = 64152$.

6. The astronaut has 1000 litres of fuel, and needs one litre of fuel for every mile driven. Hence it is not possible to travel more than 1000 miles. For *one* way of covering 1000 miles:

   (a) Fill the fuel tank and put the container with its remaining 400 litres on the buggy.

   (b) Leaving the second fuel container at the starting point, follow a circular route of 500 miles, ending back at the starting point. There is just enough fuel on board to do this.

   (c) Repeat the process using the fuel in the second container, following a different circular route.

The two routes could form a 'figure of eight' as shown:

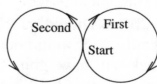

Therefore **the greatest distance that the astronaut can cover in the exploration is 1000 miles.**

1996 – 1997 Junior Solutions

1. The most direct way to measure 650ml is as follows. You need to show your steps in a similar level of detail to this for full marks, or you could use diagrams.
    Call the large jug L and the small jug S.
    (i) Fill S; pour this into L.
    (ii) Fill S; pour 150ml from this to fill L. This leaves 400 ml in S. Empty L.
    (iii) Pour the 400ml from S to L.
    (iv) Fill S; pour 300ml from this to fill L. This leaves 250ml in S. Empty L.
    (v) Pour the 250ml from S to L.
    (vi) Fill S; pour 450ml from this to fill L. This leaves 100ml in S. Empty L.
    (vii) Pour the 100ml from S to L.
    (viii) Fill S; pour all 550ml from S to L. This gives the required 650 ml in L.

    For a possible bonus mark you might consider what volumes are measurable with these jugs and what volumes are not.

2. If we assign the number 0 to A, 1 to B, 2 to C etc, then the letters of AVOCH correspond to the numbers: 0 21 14 2 and 7 which add up to 44.
    BRACO   has sum 1 + 17 + 0 + 2 + 14 = 34,
    CARRICK   has sum 2 + 0 + 17 + 17 + 8 + 2 + 10 = 56,
    DALKEITH   has sum 3 + 0 + 11 + 10 + 4 + 8 + 19 + 7 = 62 and
    EDZELL   has sum 4 + 3 + 25 + 4 + 11 + 11 = 58.
    The number for
    DALKEITH is the only one which differs from the signpost.
    Actually, the DALKEITH number would be correct if the letters A, B, C etc were represented by 1, 2, 3 etc, but then all the others would be wrong!

3. Town Hall Clock.
    At 15:20 on Thursday, the clock shows 25 minutes past 11, and it is going backwards at 55 min/hour. Saturday, at 08:20, is exactly 41 hours later, so the clock will have gone backwards by 41 × 55 minutes, i.e. by 37 hours 35 minutes. As it is a 12 hour clock, therefore the time it shows will be 1 hour 35 minutes earlier than the time it showed at 15:20 on Thursday, namely 1 hour 35 minutes earlier than 11.25.
    Therefore,
    at twenty past eight on the following Saturday morning, the Town Hall clock shows 10 minutes to 10.

4.   By-Election.

As 75% of the electorate voted and 60% of those who voted supported Sally, $0.75 \times 0.6 \times 100 = 45\%$ of the electorate supported Sally. Also, 18% of the electorate supported Bertie and 25% of the electorate did not vote. At best (ignoring the fringe candidates), the remainder of the electorate, i.e. $100 - 45 - 18 - 25 = 12$, 12%, voted for Cathy, which is less than Bertie's 18%. Thus

Bertie fared better than Cathy.

5.   Let us call the groups by their first initials, B, H, S, W. We have the information

Jack	H	B	W	S	one right
Jill	B	W	S	H	two right

Jill gave exactly two groups in their correct places; the two wrong choices must therefore be in each other's place. By leaving two of Jill's choices as they are and swapping over the other two we get six possible rearrangements: (i) BWHS (ii) BHSW (iii) BSWH (iv) HWSB (v) SWBH (vi) WBSH. We are told that H and W were not next to each other, so only (ii), (v) and (vi) work. Of these, only (vi) agrees with Jack's choice in one place.

Hence the correct winning order is:

Waterhole, Blare, Sleekit Beasties, Howling Gaels.

6.   20m lengths of track are always cheaper per metre than 15m lengths. However, since 20 does not divide exactly into 350 but leaves remainders of 10, 30, 50m etc, Dragonia Railways has to buy at least two 15m lengths. If it wants more than two lengths of 15m track, then it must buy an additional quantity that is a multiple of 20, so it can interchange any 4 lengths of 15m track with 3 lengths of 20m track. The possible amounts, with corresponding prices are therefore

Lengths of 15m track	2	6	10	14	18	22
Lengths of 20m track	16	13	10	7	4	1
Cost of 15m track	900	2550	3900	5320	6840	8360
Cost of 20m track	8000	6500	5000	3500	2000	500
Total cost	8900	9050	8900	8820	8840	8860

Thus Dragonia Railways should choose

14 lengths of 15m track and 7 of 20m track.

1995 – 1996 Junior Solutions

1. Let the number be $wxyz$, where w, x, y and z are digits. From (b) we have $z = w + x + y$ and from (c) we have $w = x + y$, hence $z = 2w$. It follows that z is even and $w < 5$. If $x = 0$, then $w = y$, since $w = x + y$, but this contradicts (a). Similarly, if $y = 0$, then $w = x$, which again contradicts (a). Hence x and y are different digits, both greater than 0. Since $w = x + y$ it follows that w is at least 3. But we have already seen that w is less than 5 and hence the only possible values of w are 3 and 4.

    If $w = 3$, then $z = 6$ and, since $w = x + y$, the digits x and y are either 1 and 2 respectively or 2 and 1 respectively. The number $wxyz$ is then 3126 or 3216. Condition (d) requires the reversal $zyxw$ to be a multiple of 7. However, neither 6213 nor 6123 is a multiple of 7. We deduce that w cannot be 3.

    Hence $w = 4$ and $z = 8$. Since $w = x + y$, the digits x and y are 1 and 3 respectively or 3 and 1 respectively (they cannot both be 2, since no two digits are the same). The number $wxyz$ is then 4138 or 4318. When reversed, 4138 is not exactly divisible by 7, but 4318 reversed is 8134, which is exactly divisible by 7 (in fact, $8134 = 7 \times 1162$). Therefore:

    the number of my bank card is 4318.

2. In a magic square, the sum of the numbers in each row equals the magic number m, the sum of the numbers in each column equals m and the sum of the numbers in each of the two main diagonals equals m. The sum of all the numbers in a 3×3 magic square is $3m$, since it is the same as the sum of the totals for the three rows (or the columns). In the given block, which is clearly not a magic square as it stands, the sum of all the numbers is 135. If we are able to rearrange the numbers in the block to form a magic square, then the sum of all the numbers will still be 135 and so the magic number will be $135 \div 3 = 45$.

    One possible arrangement of the block giving a magic square (with magic number 45) is

    $$\begin{array}{ccc} 22 & 7 & 16 \\ 9 & 15 & 21 \\ 14 & 23 & 8 \end{array}$$

    (Note that in any 3×3 magic square the number in the middle is one third of the magic number. This is true since the sum of the two diagonals and the middle row is $3m$, but these are just the two outside columns, which total $2m$, plus three times the middle entry which must therefore be $m/3$.)

    In any block taken from a month in a calendar the numbers can be represented as follows, with the middle number denoted by x:

    $$\begin{array}{ccc} x - 8 & x - 7 & x - 6 \\ x - 1 & x & x + 1 \\ x + 6 & x + 7 & x + 8 \end{array}$$

Rearrange these numbers as

$$\begin{array}{ccc} x + 7 & x - 8 & x + 1 \\ x - 6 & x & x + 6 \\ x - 1 & x + 8 & x - 7 \end{array}$$

Then the sum of each row is $3x$, the sum of each column is $3x$ and the sum of each of the two diagonals is $3x$. Therefore:

**any 3×3 block taken from one month in a calendar
can be rearranged to make a magic square.**

3. A sensible strategy in this type of problem is to identify options which cannot be true and then see what remains.

By (a), Fred is not the manager.

By (b), Fred is not the coach.

By (f), Tom is not the goalkeeper.

By (f), Jane is not the goalkeeper.

By (h), Tom is not the coach.

By (c), Susan has no brother, so by (a) she is not the manager.

By (e), Tom is in the same class as Susan, but, by (f), the goalkeeper is not, so Susan is not the goalkeeper.

	Manager	Coach	Captain	Goalkeeper
Fred	No (a)	No (b)		
Jane				No (f)
Susan	No (c,a)			No (e,f)
Tom		No (h)		No (f)

Hence Fred is the goalkeeper.

By (d), Jane is not the captain.

	Manager	Coach	Captain	Goalkeeper
Fred	No (a)	No (b)	××	Yes
Jane			No (d)	No (f)
Susan	No (c,a)			No (e,f)
Tom		No (h)		No (f)

So, Jane is either the manager or the coach, but (g) and (b) mean that Susan cannot be either manager or coach, so Susan must be the captain.

	Manager	Coach	Captain	Goalkeeper
Fred	No (a)	No (b)	××	Yes
Jane			No (d)	No (f)
Susan	No (c,a)	××	Yes	No (e,f)
Tom		No (h)	××	No (f)

So Tom has to be the manager leaving Jane as the coach.

4. The year in question was less than 195 years ago, and so it was after 1800. We are asked about what *happened* 105 years later, and so the starting year could not have been later than 1890. If it was (i) a leap year, (ii) one year after a leap year, or (iii) two years after a leap year, then by 105 years later, February 29th would have occurred 25 times (remembering that 1900 was not a leap year). However, if it was (iv) three years after a leap year, then, by 105 years later, February 29th would have occurred 26 times. (N.B. 1800 was not a leap year and so it looks as if we have forgotten 1801, 1802 and 1803 in the above. In fact, they could be included, but there is no point, since in none of these three was Christmas Day on a Wednesday.)

When Christmas Day falls on a Wednesday, December 1st falls on a Sunday. In the following year, December 1st is a Monday in a non-leap year and a Tuesday in a leap year. To find the day of the week on which December 1st falls 105 years later, add to 105 the number of occurrences of February 29th, find the remainder on division by 7 and then advance that number of days from Sunday. In cases (i), (ii) and (iii) the remainder on division of 130 (= 105 + 25) by 7 is 4, and so we deduce that December 1st is a Thursday. For case (iv) the remainder is 5 and December 1st is a Friday. In both cases, December has five Saturdays. Hence,

in December 105 years later, there were five Saturdays.

5. The comet reaches the point of intersection of the orbits after the following numbers of years:

$$3, \quad 3 + 62, \quad 3 + 2 \times 62, \quad 3 + 3 \times 62, \quad \text{etc.}$$

Each of these numbers is 3 plus an even number and so is *odd*.

The planet reaches the point of intersection after the following numbers of years:

$$8, \quad 2 \times 8, \quad 3 \times 8, \quad 4 \times 8, \quad \text{etc.}$$

Each of these numbers is even.

Hence:

the comet and the planet never meet.

6. The five sums involve the squares of all but two of the houses. The total number of terms in the sums is $2 + 3 + 4 + 5 + 6 = 20$, but since eight of the house numbers occur at least twice, the total number of houses involved is reduced by at least 8 so is at most 12. The square of every house number except mine and Mr Brown's does occur in the sums, and therefore my house number cannot be more than 14. By (v), my house number is the sum of six squares. The smallest possible sum of six different squares of integers is $1^2 + 2^2 + 3^2 + 4^2 + 5^2 + 6^2 = 91$, and the next smallest is $1^2 + 2^2 + 3^2 + 4^2 + 5^2 + 7^2 = 104$, which shows that my house number is at least 11. It follows that my house number is 11, 12, 13 or 14.

    The square of my house number is the sum of two perfect squares. The number $11^2 = 121$ is *not* the sum of two perfect squares, for if we subtract $1^2, 2^2, 3^2, \ldots, 10^2$ in turn from 11^2 we get 120, 117, 112, 105, 96, 85, 72, 57, 40, 21, none of which is a perfect square. Hence my house number is not 11. Similarly, it can be shown that my house number is not 12 and not 14. It follows that my house number is 13.

    $13^2 = 169$ is expressible as the sum of 2, 3, 4, 5 and 6 squares respectively:

    $$13^2 = 12^2 + 5^2$$
    $$13^2 = 12^2 + 4^2 + 3^2$$
    $$13^2 = 10^2 + 8^2 + 2^2 + 1^2$$
    $$13^2 = 8^2 + 7^2 + 6^2 + 4^2 + 2^2$$
    $$13^2 = 9^2 + 7^2 + 5^2 + 3^2 + 2^2 + 1^2.$$

    The numbers whose squares occur in the sums are 1, 2, 3, 4, 5, 6, 7, 8, 9, 10 and 12. Of these, 1, 3, 4, 5, 7, 8 and 12 occur twice each, and 2 occurs three times. The only number less than 13 missing is 11. This suggests that Mr Brown's house is number 11, but it must be verified that $13^2 - 11^2 = 48$ is not a sum of squares of up to five different integers, for we have not ruled out the possibility that 13^2 could be expressed as sums of two, three, four, five and six squares in other ways. In fact, it is easily checked that 48 is not a sum of squares of up to five different integers. It follows that 13^2 is not equal to 11^2 plus a sum of up to five other different squares and so 11^2 could not have occurred in any of the five sums. Hence

    Mr Brown's house number is 11.

    (Note that $13^2 = 10^2 + 7^2 + 4^2 + 2^2$. If this is taken in place of $13^2 = 10^2 + 8^2 + 2^2 + 1^2$ in the above list, then the squares of 1, 2, 3, 4, 5, 6, 7, 8, 9, 10 and 12 all occur, but only six of them occur at least twice. Thus the conditions stated in the question would not have been satisfied if we had made this choice for 13^2 instead of the choice we made.)